D1029212

**Monte Carlo
Methods**

Monte Carlo Methods

Their Role for Econometrics

V. Kerry Smith
Resources for the Future, Inc.
and
State University of New York
at Binghamton

Lexington Books
D.C. Heath and Company
Lexington, Massachusetts
Toronto   London

WILLIAM MADISON RANDALL LIBRARY UNC AT WILMINGTON

Library of Congress Cataloging in Publication Data

Smith, Vincent Kerry, 1945–
   Monte Carlo methods

   Includes bibliographical references.
   1. Monte Carlo method. 2. Econometrics.
I. Title.
HB74.M3S53   330'.01'82   72–3555
ISBN 0–669–84327-X

Copyright © 1973 by D.C. Heath and Company

All rights reserved. No part of this publication may be reproduced or transmitted in any form or by any means, electronic or mechanical, including photocopy, recording, or any information storage or retrieval system, without permission in writing from the publisher.

Published simultaneously in Canada.

Printed in the United States of America.

International Standard Book Number: 0–669–84327-X

Library of Congress Catalog Card Number: 72–3555

HB 74
·M3
·S 53

To Pauline and My Parents

141696

Table of Contents

List of Figures

List of Tables

Preface

Over the past fifteen years econometricians and statisticians have developed a research methodology for those problems which defied analytical solution with existing knowledge. Perhaps the greatest single influence upon this development was exerted by the concomitant growth in large-scale computer facilities. Today the Monte Carlo approach to evaluating estimating techniques is becoming increasingly popular. The purpose of this book is to describe, in detail, the Monte Carlo method for estimator evaluation, noting its special role for econometric research. The volume seeks to teach the methodology, critically evaluate it, summarize the state of the art in Monte Carlo findings, and present two case studies as examples.

It should be noted at the outset that the term Monte Carlo means different things to different disciplines. This book is not concerned with variance reducing techniques of simulation analysis, which rely on the reorganization of the simulation model so as to learn more of the relationship between the input and output variables involved (see [62], [63] and [114] for details). Rather, my concern is with the application of sampling experiments to the evaluation of the properties of one or more estimators. In contrast to other work reporting Monte Carlo results, the primary objective of this book is to discuss Monte Carlo as a research tool. Thus, the results of these studies, where appropriate, have been included in the review of the literature.[a]

The first chapter explains the Monte Carlo method and discusses its important role for estimation and hypothesis testing. A variety of examples serve to illustrate the philosophy and basic logic of the approach. Chapter 2 reviews the general linear model as an example of the analytical approach to the derivation of estimator properties. The exact small-sample behavior of two-stage least squares for a simple model is also developed. After a brief review of the literature in this area, the analytical and Monte Carlo approaches are compared with emphasis given to the strengths and weaknesses of each. The third chapter summarizes most of the published results of sampling experiments for econometric estimators including both single and simultaneous equation problems. Chapters 4 and 5 each present an example of a series of sampling experiments to evaluate a specific problem. Finally, Chapter 6 makes a few brief remarks about the present and future roles of the Monte Carlo method.

---

[a]The principal omission is a book by Lee, Judge, and Zellner [97] which deals with estimators for a very specific problem—the Markov Probability model.

Many individuals have contributed directly to what is good in this book. The material developed here was stimulated by my dissertation supervised by Manoranjan Dutta. He first interested me in this area and taught me econometrics and I remain in his debt. Jan Kmenta, Thomas Naylor, and Alan Powell read various chapters of this book and gave helpful advice and criticism. In addition, Charles Cicchetti contributed to this volume not only through his work with me on the material discussed in Chapter 4, but also through his encouragement and perceptive comments. Finally, I owe a very large debt to Richard Quandt who read the manuscript with remarkable alacrity, offering most-constructive suggestions. I am sure that it has been improved immeasurably as a result.

In addition, I owe more than the usual debt to my family. My mother and sister, Sharon, read the manuscript for clarity and grammar. Their contribution clearly transcends familial responsibility.

Every author owes his spouse a large debt for the patient encouragement only she can provide during the course of the work. However, my debt to my wife, Pauline, is especially great. She not only cheerfully put up with me for the duration of the study, but also typed, edited, and proofread every draft of the manuscript. Needless to say, all errors and shortcomings in the design and presentation of the study are entirely my own.

V. Kerry Smith
Washington, D.C.
September, 1972

**Monte Carlo
Methods**

1 What Is Monte Carlo?

Monte Carlo techniques are procedures which enable the economist or statistician to set up a laboratory within which the properties of the econometric estimators may be discerned. The purpose of this chapter is to describe the technique and its objectives in detail. First, it is necessary to examine the role of statistical inference for econometrics. Given the importance of such inference for decision making with incomplete information, the significance of Monte Carlo procedures for both theoretical and applied econometric research may be established. This discussion is followed by an explanation of the inductive nature of the results obtained from Monte Carlo experiments. Section 1.3 outlines the methodology with a simple two-equation example. Section 1.4 discusses the interpretation and analysis of the results and Section 1.5 summarizes the chapter.

1.1 The Problem and Its Importance

In most scientific research decisions must be made without complete information. One of the reasons for undertaking such research is to add to the available stock of knowledge. However, an important point to be recognized is that we will never have complete information for any decision. Accordingly, there are substantial advantages to be derived from the development of a logical procedure within which these decisions may be made efficiently and consistently. It is to this aim that statistics is primarily devoted. Statistical inference attempts to learn or infer more about the state of the world from the information available. There are two major areas of interest in statistics which both cooperate toward this end.

The first major concern of statistical inference is estimation. This is a method of using sample information to learn something of the nature of the underlying process which generated the information. It is generally assumed that each sample outcome is the result of a process which is composed of systematic and nonsystematic (i.e., random) influences. Moreover, the mechanism by which sample outcomes are generated is also assumed capable of description in terms of a set of one or more parameters. Estimation theory seeks to derive procedures for using sample information so as to learn what the values of these parameters are. Convention specifies that the values, which these techniques designate as the parameter values, are defined as *estimates*. The methods by which these estimates are determined from sample outcomes are labeled *estimators*.

Since the estimates are random variables as a result of their derivation from sample information, which is stochastic, each estimator can be described in terms of the distribution of its estimates. That is, if we think of selecting a large number of random samples from the same population and using each one with a given estimator, then corresponding to each sample there will be an estimate for each of the parameters of interest. The set of such estimates for a given parameter is the sampling distribution for that estimator.

This information can be used in a number of ways. One important role relates to the second major concern of statistical inference. It may be that we have some preconceived ideas of what the value of a particular parameter might be. We would like to know if our sample's outcomes are consistent with this value for the parameter. In more formal terms, our beliefs are hypotheses and the process of assessing the consistency of sample information with them is hypothesis testing. In order to test any hypothesis we must know what the distribution of our parameter estimates is, and design a test to accommodate the hypothesis. While such inference can help in the organization, interpretation, and the use of sample information it does not create a means of "filling the gap." In fact, we know the probability (for continuous random variables) that a particular estimator's estimate will exactly equal the true value of the parameter of interest is zero. However, decisions must be made and one might say statistical inference attempts to make this process as efficient as possible.

It should be clear then, that the usefulness of any estimator can only be assessed in terms of the distribution of estimates it will provide for the problem at hand. Knowledge of such a distribution allows us to make probability statements regarding the location of the true value of the parameter of concern. The same type of reasoning is fundamental to hypothesis testing. Any hypothesis is either true or false, but the decision maker does not know which is the case. If he knows the sampling distribution of the test statistic used, then it is possible to quantify the likelihood of his making particular errors. For example, he might reject a hypothesis which is true (a Type I error). Alternatively, he might accept a hypothesis which is false (a Type II error). Test statistics are designed so as to quantify these probabilities. Moreover, classical inference selects tests which minimize the probability of a Type II error.

It is important to recognize that such a discrimination process in tests, hypotheses, and estimators necessarily requires knowledge of the relevant sampling distributions. Econometric research is no different from that of any other decision oriented science. It also seeks to estimate and test economic models.[1] However, the models which are representative of economic phenomena do not always conform to those assumed for classical statistics. For example, a large segment of econometrics has been devoted to linear economic models wherein the individual equations are interdependent. In such cases, new estimation procedures and test statistics have had to be developed so that decision making might progress. For many of these problems the estimator is a detailed (and for practical purposes intractable) convolution of the distribution of the error of the model.[a] Consequently, most descriptions of the characteristics of these estimators have been confined to their large sample (asymptotic) properties. Since small, rather than large, data sets are fequently all that are available in applied econometrics, these asymptotic properties are not particularly helpful. The negligent use of asymptotic distribution functions for these estimators, when the margin of error resulting from limitations on the sample size is unknown, converts reasoned inference to guesswork.

The complex nature of most econometric models, and the large number of structural parameters necessary to describe the distribution functions for the econometric estimators have been primary reasons for the slow progress in deriving exact distributions. Nonetheless, Basmann [7], Richardson [140], Sawa [147], and Takeuchi [167] have made important strides in this area.[b] However, the models used in their research have had to remain at very simple levels. Moreover, in some cases the problems are simply intractable from a mathematical viewpoint.

It is important to recognize that inference in econometrics is dependent upon a knowledge of estimator and test statistic properties under the sampling conditions usually experienced. Accordingly, there is substantial incentive for looking to other approaches for obtaining some information on the properties of the tools of inference in econometrics.

1.2 Philosophy and Objectives of the Monte Carlo Approach

One approach for obtaining information on the small sample properties of these econometric tools is through recourse to experimentation. That is, the performance of the estimation methods (and test statistics) is assessed by examining a iarge array of cases in which the "state of the world" or frame of reference is under the control of the experimenter. Monte Carlo techniques construct a hypothetical "world" so that samples may be provided for the estimators to work with. In so doing, the experimenter can learn more of each estimator's probability distribution of parameter estimates for a given model. Thus, Monte Carlo techniques, as they are applied in econometrics, represent procedures for using statistical inference to evaluate the tools used in estimation and testing. There may seem to be some circularity in this statement (i.e., using the techniques of

---

[a]Chapter 2 provides some simple examples of how particular estimator's sampling distributions may be derived from that of the error.

[b]See Chapter 2, Section 2.3, for a summary of the findings of these studies.

inference to evaluate the techniques of inference) and it is because of this that particular attention must be given to the analysis of data derived from Monte Carlo studies.

Through the experimental approach, we obtain a sample from each estimator's underlying probability distribution of parameter estimates (or from a test's distribution of test statistics) and then seek to learn about the process which provided the sample. However, that process is the estimating technique. All other influences in a Monte Carlo experiment are controlled and therefore known.

Monte Carlo experiments provide us with several additional abilities. (1) They can be used to provide reproducible knowledge concerning the accuracy of parameter estimates. (2) While such experiments cannot tell whether there is a cause and effect relationship between two variables, they can aid in the construction of confidence intervals in causal prediction.[2] (3) They can be extremely useful as a teaching device. Basic concepts in statistics and econometrics, such as the central limit theorem, can be demonstrated using the Monte Carlo methodology (see Patton [129]). (4) Finally, they provide the means of assessing the sensitivity of particular models' results, especially stochastic ones, to the assumptions underlying their construction.

The Monte Carlo procedure for estimator evaluation is essentially an inductive approach. We seek to infer estimator properties from observed behavior in a controlled setting. Consequently, our answers will not be true or false. Rather, they are established only in probabilistic terms. Consider the following example. We wish to select the "best" estimator for the variance of a given variable. Two estimators are available

Table 1.1
Estimators for Population Variance[a]

Observation	Samples		
	1	2	3
1	11.6	16.1	6.2
2	7.6	18.8	6.8
3	21.9	−8.0	4.1
4	17.2	−0.1	6.9
5	20.9	20.7	20.9
Sample Mean	15.8	10.5	9.0
s_1^2	31.3	108.7	36.2
s_2^2	39.1	135.9	45.3
$\lvert \sigma^2 - s_1^2 \rvert$	68.7	8.7	63.8
$\lvert \sigma^2 - s_2^2 \rvert$	60.9	35.9	54.7

[a]The values of the estimated means and variances have been rounded to one significant digit to the right of the decimal place. The observations are in thousands of dollars.

$$s_1^{\ 2} = \frac{1}{n} \sum_i (x_i - \bar{x})^2 \ \text{ or } \ s_2^{\ 2} = \frac{1}{n-1} \sum_i (x_i - \bar{x})^2,$$

where

n = sample size, $\bar{x}$ = sample mean.

One approach for evaluating the two would consist in examining their performance with samples from a population with a known variance. For example, if we know that in a certain town the mean income is seven thousand dollars and the variance (σ^2) is one hundred then we might randomly select samples from all the families of the town, and apply each estimator. For the sake of simplicity, suppose we selected three samples each with five families.[c] Table 1.1 provides the sample values for the family incomes, the samples means, and the two estimates of the variance. In addition, the absolute value of the deviation between the known variance and our respective estimates of it has been computed. In two of the three samples, the second estimator is closer to the true value than the first. However, in both cases the techniques understimate the true value of the variance. In the remaining sample the first estimator comes closest to the true value. Clearly, there are not enough cases presented to generalize upon. For the sake of example, we will confine our attention only to the information we have. On the basis of it, using the criteria of absolute proximity per sample, we would conclude that $s_2^{\ 2}$ is a "better" estimator than $s_1^{\ 2}$.[d] However, we cannot be really sure. This doubt is, perhaps, clearer in our example, than if a large number of cases with different sample sizes and different underlying characteristics of the population had been used. Nonetheless, even with the most extensive experimentation our answers are not certain.

By way of contrast, another approach to solving this problem would have been to examine the expected value of each estimator. If we let $\mu = E(x_i)$ then we can write the equation for $s_1^{\ 2}$ as in (1.1):

$$s_1^{\ 2} = \frac{1}{n} \sum_i [(x_i - \mu) - (\bar{x} - \mu)]^2 \tag{1.1}$$

Expanding (1.1) and making use of the rules for working with the summation operator (1.1) may be written as (1.2):

---

[c]The samples are assumed to be simple random samples of the underlying population of families. If one actually chose this approach, a much larger number of samples as well as observations within a sample would be necessary.

[d]It should be noted that this criteria does not take account of the total magnitude of the discrepancies. For example, if we had selected the criteria minimum sum of absolute deviations as our objective function, then s_1^2 would have been the "better" technique.

$$s_1^2 = \frac{1}{n} \sum_i (x_i - \mu)^2 - (\bar{x} - \mu)^2 \qquad (1.2)$$

If we take the expected value of (1.2) we have:

$$E(s_1^2) = \sigma^2 - \frac{1}{n} \sigma^2 \qquad (1.3)$$

Accordingly, we *know* that the s_1^2 estimator is based, and will, on average, deviate from the true value of the variance by $- (1/n) \sigma^2$.

It is a straightforward operation to derive the expected value of s_2^2 as given. in Equation (1.4).

$$E(s_2^2) = \frac{n}{n-1} E(s_1^2) = \sigma^2 \qquad (1.4)$$

Fortunately, our previous example and the analytical approach concur in the choice of estimator. It is important to recognize that the preceding argument has proved that s_2^2 is better than s_1^2. Our experimental findings cannot provide such definite results. Accordingly, one might compare the two approaches in the same manner that logical arguments are classified into the inductive and deductive arguments. The latter are either valid or invalid depending upon the argument. The former can provide only probabilistic answers.

This example also serves to demonstrate another important component of the process of estimator evaluation. In essence, it illustrates the importance of the criteria we use to evaluate the techniques. This decision is equivalent to defining the loss function within which the estimators may be reviewed. A *loss function* is merely the negative of the decision maker's utility function. It is to be interpreted as the loss he encounters when he selects a particular technique and its corresponding estimate, say $\hat{\theta}$, when the true value of the parameter is θ. Clearly, the objective behind the selection process is to choose a technique which will minimize this loss.

Since the evaluative criteria is dependent upon how an estimator's estimates will be used, those sampling experiments which have evaluated several techniques report the findings with a variety of the criteria.

1.3   An Example of the Monte Carlo Methodology

Another means of explaining the Monte Carlo methodology in econometrics is via example. Consider the following two-equation linear simultaneous model.

Both equations will be identified, if the values of γ_{11} and γ_{22} are nonzero and the values for γ_{12} and γ_{21} are zero.[e]

$$\beta_{11} Y_{1t} + \beta_{12} Y_{2t} + \gamma_{11} Z_{1t} + \gamma_{12} Z_{2t} = U_{1t} \qquad (1.5)$$

$$\beta_{21} Y_{1t} + \beta_{22} Y_{2t} + \gamma_{21} Z_{1t} + \gamma_{22} Z_{2t} = U_{2t} \qquad (1.6)$$

The Y_i's are the endogenous variables, the Z_i's are the predetermined variables, and the U_i's are random errors. The first step is to specify the "true" structure of the model given in Equations (1.5) and (1.6). In so doing, we must recognize the importance of the identification problem and the normalization rule imposed upon each equation.[3] While at this stage we shall assign values to the coefficients remaining (after accounting for the preceding considerations), there is some evidence to suggest that the numerical values should not be arbitrarily specified.[4]

Assume:

$$\beta_{11} = \bar{\beta}_1 \qquad \beta_{12} = 1 \qquad \gamma_{11} = \bar{\gamma}_1 \qquad \gamma_{12} = 0$$

$$\beta_{22} = \bar{\beta}_2 \qquad \beta_{21} = 1 \qquad \gamma_{22} = \bar{\gamma}_2 \qquad \gamma_{21} = 0$$

The presence of Z_1 in Equation (1.5) and its absence in Equation (1.6) identifies (1.6). Similarly the presence of Z_2 in (1.6) and its absence from (1.5) identifies (1.5) for this model. In matrix notation the model would appear as follows:

$$\begin{bmatrix} \bar{\beta}_1 & 1 \\ 1 & \bar{\beta}_2 \end{bmatrix} \begin{bmatrix} Y_{1t} \\ Y_{2t} \end{bmatrix} + \begin{bmatrix} \bar{\gamma}_1 & 0 \\ 0 & \bar{\gamma}_2 \end{bmatrix} \begin{bmatrix} Z_{1t} \\ Z_{2t} \end{bmatrix} = \begin{bmatrix} U_{1t} \\ U_{2t} \end{bmatrix} \qquad (1.7)$$

In order to use this model to provide the hypothetical data used in estimator evaluation, it is necessary to solve for the reduced form. Consequently, the endogenous coefficient matrix must be nonsingular. In this example the solution is straightforward.

---

[e]The restrictions used to identify these equations are of the exclusion type and are members of the class of linear homogenous restrictions. When these are used, the order condition for identification requires that the number of predetermined variables (Z's) excluded from the equation in question be equal to or greater than the included endogenous variables (Y's) less one. For this model in Equation (1.5) # of excluded predetermined = 1; # of included endogenous = 2; $1 \geqslant 2 - 1$. See Fisher [51] for details.

$$
\begin{bmatrix} Y_{1t} \\ Y_{2t} \end{bmatrix} = - \begin{bmatrix} \dfrac{\bar{\beta}_2\,\bar{\gamma}_1}{\bar{\beta}_2\,\bar{\beta}_1 - 1} & \dfrac{-\bar{\gamma}_1}{\bar{\beta}_2\,\bar{\beta}_1 - 1} \\[3mm] \dfrac{-\bar{\gamma}_1}{\bar{\beta}_2\,\bar{\beta}_1 - 1} & \dfrac{\bar{\beta}_1\,\bar{\gamma}_2}{\bar{\beta}_2\,\bar{\beta}_1 - 1} \end{bmatrix} \begin{bmatrix} Z_{1t} \\ Z_{2t} \end{bmatrix}
$$

$$
+
$$

$$
\begin{bmatrix} \dfrac{\bar{\beta}_2}{\bar{\beta}_2\,\bar{\beta}_1 - 1} & \dfrac{-1}{\bar{\beta}_1\,\bar{\beta}_2 - 1} \\[3mm] \dfrac{-1}{\bar{\beta}_2\,\bar{\beta}_1 - 1} & \dfrac{\bar{\beta}_1}{\bar{\beta}_2\,\bar{\beta}_1 - 1} \end{bmatrix} \begin{bmatrix} U_{1t} \\ U_{2t} \end{bmatrix} \tag{1.8}
$$

There are two final components which are necessary to simulate this model and thereby provide the hypothetical data used in our Monte Carlo studies. First, a set of values for the predetermined variables (Z_1 and Z_2) must be given. In order to satisfy the assumptions of the model, they should be uncorrelated with the errors (U_1 and U_2). Second, the errors must be provided. Before discussing their derivation, it is important to recognize the procedure given all information.

The model is used to generate a set of samples of preassigned size. The only inputs to the simulation which change across this set are the random errors. Each sample in the set has a series of values of the random errors which are independent of those of any other set. Typically, the values for the predetermined variables and structural coefficients remain constant. This set of samples then constitutes *one* experiment. If we wish to examine the effect of variations in the magnitudes of the structural coefficients or in the collinearity between Z_1 and Z_2 or any other factor, then additional experiments must be constructed for each set of initial conditions. These conditions do not change across the samples of a given experiment. Corresponding to each set of initial conditions is a different population for Y_1 and Y_2.

Returning to the random errors of the model, there are several important aspects of their derivation. First, they are not "truly" random numbers, but rather numbers which satisfy the statistical properties of a random variable. Consequently, they are designated *pseudorandom numbers*. Naylor [119] describes the properties of an ideal pseudorandom number generator as yielding sequences of numbers that are: " . . . (1) uniformly distributed, (2) statistically independent, (3) reproducible, and (4) nonrepeating for any desired length. Furthermore, such a generator should also be capable of (5) generating random numbers at high rates of speed, yet of (6) requiring a minimum amount of computer memory capacity."[5] These numbers are transformed so as to conform to the distributional assumptions for the model under study.[6]

One important problem in generating numbers for econometric models is transforming random variables generated under the assumption of independent, normal distributions with zero mean and unitary variance. Typically, econometric models have errors with other than unitary variance and nonzero covariances between the errors. Accordingly, it is important to consider a procedure for the transformation of numbers from independent normally distributed random variables, to values which would have come from multivariate normal distributions with variance–covariance matrix of Σ and expected values of zero.

In the example let us assume that the covariance matrix is given in (1.9).

$$\Sigma = \begin{bmatrix} \sigma_{11}^2 & \sigma_{12} \\ \sigma_{12} & \sigma_{22}^2 \end{bmatrix} \tag{1.9}$$

Further, assume that we have generated two sequences of random numbers from independent normal distributions with zero means and unit variances. Nagar [117] has provided a procedure for transforming such numbers into values in conformity with the assumed error structure for U_1 and U_2. Equation (1.10) provides the transformation for the tth value of U_1 and U_2, given e_1 and e_2 are values from independent standardized normal distributions.

$$[U_{1t}\ U_{2t}] = [e_{1t}\ e_{2t}] \begin{bmatrix} s_{11} & 0 \\ s_{21} & s_{22} \end{bmatrix} \tag{1.10}$$

The covariance structure of U_1 and U_2 is known and can be shown to be expressed in terms of the transformation matrix.[7]

$$\Sigma = \begin{bmatrix} s_{11} & s_{21} \\ 0 & s_{22} \end{bmatrix} \begin{bmatrix} s_{11} & 0 \\ s_{21} & s_{22} \end{bmatrix} = \begin{bmatrix} s_{11}^2 + s_{21}^2 & s_{21}\,s_{22} \\ s_{22}\,s_{21} & s_{22}^2 \end{bmatrix} \tag{1.11}$$

Accordingly we know that:

$$s_{22} = +\sqrt{\sigma_{22}^2}$$

$$s_{21} = \sigma_{12}/s_{22}$$

$$s_{11} = +\sqrt{\sigma_{11}^2 - s_{21}^2}$$

The procedure is easily generalized to a many-equation system. However, the co-variance matrix must be nonsingular, as the form of the joint density function for the multivariate case might suggest.[8]

In order to further illustrate the procedure, consider the following numer-ical example:

$$\beta_{11} = \bar{\beta}_1 = 0.5 \qquad\qquad \gamma_{11} = \bar{\gamma}_1 = 0.1$$

$$\beta_{22} = \bar{\beta}_2 = 0.2 \qquad\qquad \gamma_{22} = \bar{\gamma}_2 = 0.4$$

The reduced form coefficients of Equation (1.8) are given in (1.12)

$$\begin{bmatrix} Y_{1t} \\ Y_{2t} \end{bmatrix} = \begin{bmatrix} 0.022 & -0.444 \\ -0.111 & 0.222 \end{bmatrix} \begin{bmatrix} Z_{1t} \\ Z_{2t} \end{bmatrix} + \begin{bmatrix} -0.222 & 1.111 \\ 1.111 & -0.555 \end{bmatrix} \begin{bmatrix} U_{1t} \\ U_{2t} \end{bmatrix} \qquad (1.12)$$

If we assume that the variance–covariance matrix for the structural errors is given by (1.13), then it is a straightforward matter to transform independent standard-ized normal deviates ($\mu = 0$, $\sigma^2 = 1$) into the desired form.

$$\Sigma = \begin{bmatrix} 9.0 & 0 \\ 0 & 16.0 \end{bmatrix} \qquad (1.13)$$

Equation (1.14) provides the prerequisite linear transformation.

$$[U_{1t}\ U_{2t}] = [e_{1t}\ e_{2t}] \begin{bmatrix} 3.0 & 0 \\ 0 & 4.0 \end{bmatrix} \qquad (1.14)$$

In order to complete the example suppose that Z_{1t} is a trend variable (e.g., $t = 1, 2, \ldots$) and Z_{2t} is a dichotomous variable, then Table 1.2 provides the corresponding solutions for Y_{1t} and Y_{2t} for five observations. Each of the sets of standard normal deviates are converted using Equation (1.14) so their variance–covariance structure corresponds to (1.13). The values are then substi-tuted in (1.12) along with the values of the predetermined variables and the results are the values of the endogenous variables.

For estimator evaluation the values of the endogenous and predetermined variables are the only given information. The objective is to attempt to estimate the underlying structure. If we assume that the sample size of five is what will be

Table 1.2
Example Simulation with a Linear Model[a]

obs	Dependent Variables		Predetermined Variables		Structural Errors		Standard[b] Normal Deviates	
	Y_1	Y_2	Z_1	Z_2	U_1	U_2	e_1	e_2
1	3.9	0.05	1	1	2.0	4.3	0.665	1.075
2	-8.8	5.2	2	0	1.0	-7.8	0.340	-1.955
3	4.0	-2.3	3	1	0.0	3.9	0.008	0.985
4	-2.7	0.9	4	0	0.3	-1.9	0.110	-0.486
5	-3.8	6.4	5	0	3.9	-2.7	1.297	-0.679

[a]These values for the dependent variables and structural errors have been rounded to one significant digit to the right of the decimal.
[b]These values were obtained from *A Million Random Digits and One Hundred Thousand Deviates* (Santa Monica: Rand Corporation, 1950) as reprinted in J. Kmenta, *Elements of Econometrics* (New York: The MacMillan Co., 1971).

examined (although realistically this size is too small), then Table 1.2 presents *one* sample of a given experiment. In order to provide sufficient information from which to infer estimator properties, the number of such samples is characteristically fifty or more. In the generation of succeeding samples for this experiment, *only* the values of errors change. Thus, five different (and independent) sets of standard normal deviates would be required for the second sample, and so on, up to fifty or more samples.

The majority of the Monte Carlo studies in econometrics have, as the next step, applied each technique to the same set of samples. The result of these applications is a number of sets of parameter estimates for each technique. The exact number of sets corresponds to the number of samples. These sets of estimates constitute a sample from each technique's exact finite sample density function corresponding to the model under study. The nature of the application of the estimators (i.e., all to the same set of samples) implies that these samples are *not* independent across estimating techniques. Accordingly, the choice and interpretation of summary statistics used to characterize each estimator's properties must recognize this limitation.

1.4 Statistical Summaries of Monte Carlo Results

There are at least four areas in which the results of a Monte Carlo experiment may be profitably utilized. First, there is interest in the properties of a given estimator. That is, we would like to learn as much as possible of the character of the exact finite density function of the technique with a given parameter. Thus, some measures of central tendency and dispersion are essential information. Estimates of higher order moments may also be useful in characterizing the skewness and peakedness of the distribution. Finally, we might want to compare the sampling distribution with one or more probability distributions in order to infer similarities or differences on the basis of the sample data. In Figure 1.1, a hypothetical density function labeled E_1 (n), representing the exact finite sample density function for an estimator of the parameter θ, is presented. By the nature of the diagram we see that it is centered at the true value of the parameter. Moreover, the tails of the distribution are somewhat "thick." Our sample information from Monte Carlo studies seeks to provide some of these observations as one of its primary objectives.

Secondly, the results of Monte Carlo experiments can be used to compare the effects of "changes in the environment" on a given estimator with a given parameter. For example, there is frequently interest in the speed of convergence of the exact finite distribution of an estimator to its asymptotic counterpart. Consequently, comparisons between the results with a given model and estimator but with different sample sizes may help to provide us some of these answers.[f]

---

[f]See Chapter 4 for a discussion of these results.

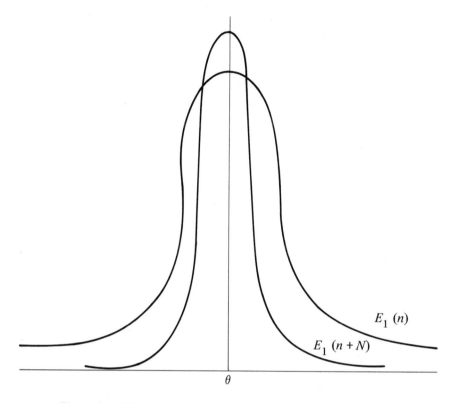

Figure 1.1. Effect of Sample Size upon the Density Function for a Hypothetical Estimator.

Moreover, the rules of inference derived under asymptotic conditions may be shown to be usable for certain threshold sample sizes. In terms of Figure 1.1, again, the comparisons sought under this objective are similar to that exhibited in a comparison of the two hypothetical distributions $E_1(n)$ and $E_1(n + N)$. This example illustrates the familiar property of many exact finite distributions, namely, concentration of the density function about the true value, θ, with increases in the sample size (i.e., from n to $n + N$).

A third use of Monte Carlo results is to compare several of the estimators of given parameter and attempt to evaluate their relative performance. Suppose that we have two estimators of a given parameter, θ, designated $E_1(m)$ and $E_2(m)$. We would like to discriminate between these two techniques and select the "best" one according to a preassigned objective function. In Figure 1.2 we have graphed one possibility. In this case, $E_1(m)$ is centered at the true value but highly dispersed, while $E_2(m)$ is biased (e.g., its density function is centered at A, bias $= A - \theta$) but has a much smaller dispersion. If a loss function is defined, then explicit choice between estimators can be made based upon the effects of these characteristics upon that loss function.

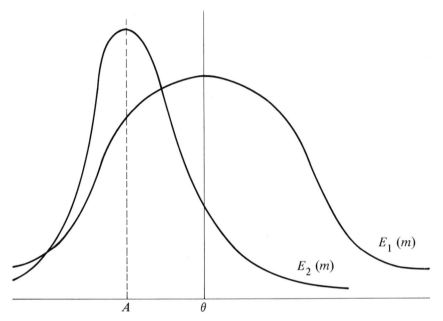

Figure 1.2. Comparison of the Density Functions of Two Hypothetical Estimators.

The fourth and final objective we shall consider consists of comparing the performance of the techniques across parameters of a multiparameter model. For example, the two-equation model previously cited had seven structural parameters which might be discussed. Four of these were structural coefficients (β_1, β_2, γ_1, and γ_2) and three were elements of the structural error's variance–covariance matrix (σ_1^2, σ_2^2, σ_{12}). Attention might focus upon the estimators' relative performance with each parameter. Alternatively, the characteristics of a given technique across structural parameters might be of primary interest. In fact, there are any number of combinations of parameter, estimator, and experimental variation which might be examined.[9]

The nature of the design of our Monte Carlo experiments affects the extent to which, and the means whereby we can examine each of the aforementioned possible objectives. The first objective may be the easiest to discuss.[g] There are a number of measures of performance of a given estimator for a specific parameter. Some of the more popular include: mean, median, or bias as measures of central tendency; variance, mean squared error, range, interquartile range, or mean sum of absolute deviations as measures of dispersion; higher order sample moments as measures of distribution's shape, and a number of others.[h] The

---

[g]It is, however, necessary to consider the model under study and whether or not exact finite moments of the estimators exist. See Chapter 2 for further discussion.

[h]See Appendix B for definitions of each.

choice of a subset of these descriptive statistics is equivalent to the definition of a loss function.

For the second objective we are concerned with comparisons across experiments for a given estimator of a specific parameter or parameters. In most cases the experimental design permits statistical testing. However, the samples must be independent across the experiments and appeal made to the central limit theorem.[10]

For the last two objectives the samples of parameter estimates for each technique are not independent. Consequently, the traditional parametric statistics used for inference are not applicable. In many cases, nonparametric (i.e., distribution-free) tests are employed in an effort to discern differences across either techniques or parameters. The tests in these cases are generally less powerful than the parametric ones. Moreover, the results of these tests are frequently not as clearcut.

This discussion does not imply that one could not design experiments within which the more traditional tools of inference were applicable. Rather, these statements refer to most of the Monte Carlo literature in econometrics. The number of parameters as well as the potential variations in the models themselves limit the feasibility of these exercises.

A final aspect of Monte Carlo results, which will be discussed in more detail in Chapter 2, relates to their generality. The results of each Monte Carlo experiment refer *only* to the model chosen. Accordingly, generalizations of the conclusions to a broad range of potential applications are not necessarily valid. Therefore, a large number of representative experiments must be conducted before the results of any Monte Carlo exercise can provide more general information.

1.5 Summary

Monte Carlo studies are important to the development of statistical inference (i.e., estimation and hypothesis testing) in econometrics, under small sample conditions. This chapter has summarized the technique and discussed the interpretation of results to be derived from it. Several points may be worthy of repetition.

(1) Applied econometrics typically has limited data sets. The use of asymptotic distribution theory in such applications, when the margin of error resulting from the sample size limitations is unknown, converts inference to guesswork.

(2) Monte Carlo techniques evaluate the performance of estimation methods through a process of experimentation in which the "frame of reference" is controlled. As a result, a sample from each estimator's underlying exact finite sample density function is obtained.

(3) The steps involved in conducting a Monte Carlo study are:

i.   Specify a true structure for the model of interest and a series of values for
      the exogenous variables.
ii.   Generate a series of pseudorandom numbers from a preassigned distribution
      (i.e., numbers satisfying the statistical properties of a random variable).
iii. Solve the model with the "givens" (i.e., structural parameters and exogenous
      variables) and the errors for the endogenous variables for a given sample
      size.
iv.   Repeat the process for a number of samples, changing only the errors.
v.   Apply the techniques of interest to each of the generated samples.
vi.   Evaluate the estimates for each technique.

(4) Four possible areas of interest for the results of Monte Carlo studies are:

i.   Properties of a given estimator with a given parameter.
ii.   Properties of a given estimator with a given paramater under different
      "given" conditions (such as sample size, error structures, etc.)
iii. Relative performance of different techniques with the same parameter,
      model, and frame of reference.
iv.   Relative performance of a given technique with different parameters of a
      given model and frame of reference.

(5) Monte Carlo experimental results refer only to the models which have
been used. Generalizations beyond this framework require extensive testing and
systematic variation in the characteristics of that environment.

Notes

1. Johnston [70] p. 5 makes this point very clearly in the second edition of
    his text. He notes: "The essential role of econometrics is the estimation and
    testing of economic models."
2. Mosbaek and Wold [113], pp. 93–95.
3. See: Chow [15], pp. 532–533; Fisher [51].
4. See: Smith [155], pp. 35–46.
5. Naylor [119], pp. 381–382.
6. See: Appendix A and Naylor, Balintfy, and Burdick and Chu [120] for a
    discussion of the conversion procedures.
7. Nagar [117], pp. 428–430. In the case of multivariate normally distributed
    errors, the covariance matrix, Σ, must be of full rank.
8. See: Mood and Graybill [110], pp. 207–215.
9. See: Sasser [146].
10. See: Smith and Patton [162].

2 The Logic of Analytical Solutions

In the Preface it was noted that the purpose of this book is to explain Monte Carlo work in econometrics. Thus, we hope to explain the methodology, summarize the results, and present examples of Monte Carlo experiments with single and multiple equation models. In order to better understand the technique and its objectives, some knowledge of alternative means of deriving information on the estimators is important. This chapter illustrates the analytical approach using the well-known results of the general linear model for a simple case. The model is generalized to a two-equation case and the resulting properties of ordinary least-squares and two-stage least squares estimators discussed. After a review of the findings of analytical studies of the simultaneous equations estimators and approximation methods for deriving estimator properties, the results and limitations of the analytical and Monte Carlo approaches are briefly compared. We find they should not be considered competitors, but rather complements.

2.1 The General Linear Model: An Example of the Analytical Approach

Most econometrics texts[1] begin their discussion of problems of estimation with a review of the classical linear model of statistical estimation theory. This example forms a "springboard" to the problems associated with estimating systems of linear equations. This same approach is also a useful outline for understanding the derivation and meaning of analytical results describing estimator properties.

Consider a simple two-variable linear model as given in Equation (2.1).

$$Y_{1t} = \alpha_1 Y_{2t} + U_t \tag{2.1}$$

This relationship describes how Y_{1t} is related to Y_{2t}. The usual assumptions made in the analysis of this model are as follows. First, the term U_t is a random error with expectation of zero and constant variance for all t. Second, U_t is not related to any other error U_{t-j}, where $j \neq 0$. Moreover, the independent variable, Y_{2t}, is not related to U_t. The coefficient, α_1, is a fixed constant which in practice is unknown. Finally, Y_2 has finite variance over the sample period. These

17

assumptions may be expressed in more familiar mathematical form as in Equation (2.2).[a]

$$\text{i. } E(U_t) \qquad\qquad = 0 \qquad\qquad \text{for all } t$$

$$\text{i.i. } E(U_t^2) \qquad\qquad = \sigma^2 \qquad\qquad \text{for all } t$$

$$\text{i.i.i. } E(U_t U_s) \qquad\qquad = E(U_t)E(U_s) \quad \text{for } s \neq t$$

$$\text{i.v. } E(U_t Y_{2t}) \qquad\qquad = 0 \qquad\qquad \text{for all } t$$

$$\text{v. } \frac{1}{n}\sum_t (Y_{2t} - \bar{Y}_2)^2 < \infty \tag{2.2}$$

The ordinary least squares (hereafter OLS) estimator selects the estimate of α_1 so as to minimize the sum of squared residuals. Since all elementary econometrics texts derive the estimator for this simple case as well as for multiple regressor models, we shall state the estimator in Equation (2.3)[b]

$$a_1 = \frac{\sum_t Y_{1t} Y_{2t}}{\sum_t Y_{2t}^2} \tag{2.3}$$

where:

a_1 = the OLS estimate of α_1 and the limits of the summation correspond to the sample space.

Before deriving the properties of the OLS estimator *for this model,*[c] some preliminary definitions are necessary. If we rewrite the estimator somewhat, it will become clear that a_1 is a linear function of the values of the dependent variable (i.e., Y_{1t}).

---

[a]The word assumptions has been italicized to emphasize that these conditions are what we presume to be true. There is no guarantee that they will be upheld in real-world data sets. Consequently the general linear model has been studied under alternative sets of assumptions describing frequently observed "real-world" conditions.

It should be reiterated that with Monte Carlo methods, our hypothetical data is based upon assumptions, in much the same way, and we control through the generation of the data the degree to which usual assumptions are upheld.

[b]See Note 1 for the citations on this derivation in several introductory texts.

[c]In actual fact the properties to be discussed refer to both single and multiple regressor linear models, so long as the assumptions of the model are upheld.

$$d_t = \frac{Y_{2t}}{\sum_t Y_{2t}^2} \tag{2.4}$$

Assumption i.v. assures that Y_{2t} is a fixed mathematical variable and therefore the d_t constructions are weights which will be used in combining the values of Y_{1t} to form the OLS estimate of α_1.[d] That is:

$$a_1 = \sum_t d_t Y_{1t} \tag{2.5}$$

There are two determinants of the properties of the OLS estimator. First, the characteristics of the weights, d_t, and second, the nature of the dependent variable Y_{1t}. Several relationships with the d_t's can be readily derived.

$$\sum d_t Y_{2t} = \sum \left[\frac{Y_{2t}}{\sum Y_{2t}^2} Y_{2t} \right] = \frac{\sum Y_{2t}^2}{\sum Y_{2t}^2} = 1 \tag{2.6a}$$

$$\sum d_t^2 = \sum \left[\frac{Y_{2t}}{\sum Y_{2t}^2} \right]^2 = \frac{\sum Y_{2t}^2}{(\sum Y_{2t}^2)^2} = \frac{1}{\sum Y_{2t}^2} \tag{2.6b}$$

With the characteristics derived for d_t in (2.6a) and (2.6b) and our assumptions concerning Y_{1t} and its components stated in Equation (2.2), it is possible to discuss the character of a_1.

Rewrite Equation (2.5) substituting Y_{1t} so that we can learn something of the central tendency of the distribution of a_1.[e]

$$a_1 = \sum d_t (\alpha_1 Y_{2t} + U_t)$$

$$= \alpha_1 \sum d_t Y_{2t} + \sum d_t U_t \tag{2.7a}$$

Making use of (2.6a) we have:

$$a_1 = \alpha_1 + \sum d_t U_t \tag{2.7b}$$

Taking the expected value of this expression and making use of assumption i.v. in (2.2), we find the well-known result that the expected value of the OLS estimator is equal to the true value.

Rearranging terms in (2.7b) somewhat, we can describe the variance in a_1 in (2.8).

---

[d]Assume hereafter that the sum is over all t.

[e]a_1 is a random variable because it is a linear function of a random variable, Y_{1t}. Under certain conditions to be explained in more detail the precise distribution of a_1 may be derived if that of Y_{1t} is known.

$$E (a_1 - \alpha_1)^2 = E \ [(\Sigma \ d_t \ U_t)^2] \tag{2.8}$$

Assumptions i.i., i.i.i., and i.v. allow us to eliminate the cross-product terms in the squared term on the right-hand side of (2.8) and find that the variance in a_1 may be written as:[f]

$$\text{Var} \ (a_1) = \Sigma \ d_t^{\ 2} \ \sigma^2 = \frac{\sigma^2}{\Sigma \ Y_{2t}^{\ 2}} \quad \text{(using 2.6b)} \tag{2.9}$$

Both the central tendency and the variance in the distribution of a_1 have been derived without appeal to asymptotic distribution theory.[2] However, at this point we do not have an idea of the form of the distribution. One approach for obtaining more information would be to examine additional moments in the distribution of a_1 for some indication.[3]

Alternatively, if we know something of the distribution of Y_{1t}, then the fact that a_1 is a linear function of the Y_{1t}'s may help in the analysis of its distribution. Traditionally, U_t is assumed to have a normal distribution and therefore Y_{1t} also has a normal distribution (given the assumptions of the model).[4] The normality of Y_{1t} is most important to hypothesis testing with linear models. It can be shown that the sum of a finite number of independent (by assumption i.i.i.) normally-distributed random variables is normally distributed.[5] This result enables us to completely describe the behavior of a_1. However, it is based upon the assumptions of our model. An alteration in some of these assumptions will most definitely affect the distribution of a_1. This proposition is generally true for all analytical studies. Their results relate to the assumed model only. Generalizations beyond the scope of the model have no basis in fact.

Consider one such example, let Y_{1t} and Y_{2t} be further related in Equation (2.10). x_t is assumed to be exogenous and to have finite variance over the sample period. Moreover, it is not related to U_t.

$$Y_{2t} = Y_{1t} + x_t \tag{2.10}$$

Y_{2t} no longer satisfies all the assumptions made in (2.2). Specifically, Equation (2.10) makes Y_{2t} a function of U_t and therefore i.v. cannot hold. Accordingly, we must reevaluate the properties derived for a_1.

In order to do so, we must first solve Equations (2.1) and (2.10) so that Y_{1t} and Y_{2t} are expressed as functions solely of x_t and U_t (i.e., derive the reduced form equations). The results are given in (2.11a) and (2.11b).

---

[f]For example, suppose $t = 1,2$ then $E \ (\Sigma d_t \ U_t)^2 = E \ [d_1^{\ 2} \ U_1^{\ 2} + 2d_1 \ d_2 \ U_1 \ U_2 + d_2^{\ 2} \ U_2^{\ 2}]$. The expected value of a sum is equal to the sum of their expectations. Consequently: $E \ [d_1^{\ 2} \ U_1^{\ 2} + 2d_1 \ d_2 \ U_1 \ U_2 + d_2^{\ 2} \ U_2^{\ 2}] = E \ [d_1^{\ 2} \ U_1^{\ 2}] + E \ [2d_1 \ d_2 \ U_1 \ U_2] + E \ [d_2^{\ 2} \ U_2^{\ 2}]$ Given assumption i.i.i., the cross-product term is zero and with i.i. and i.v. the expression is $d_1^{\ 2} \ \sigma^2 + d_2^{\ 2} \ \sigma^2$.

$$Y_{1t} = \frac{\alpha_1}{1 - \alpha_1} x_t + \frac{1}{1 - \alpha_1} U_t \qquad (2.11a)$$

$$Y_{2t} = \frac{1}{1 - \alpha_1} x_t + \frac{1}{1 - \alpha_1} U_t \qquad (2.11b)$$

Substituting into Equation (2.3), we derive an expression for the OLS estimate of α_1.

$$a_1 = \frac{\alpha_1 \Sigma x_t^2 + \Sigma x_t U_t + \alpha_1 \Sigma x_t U_t + \Sigma U_t^2}{\Sigma x_t^2 + 2 \Sigma x_t U_t + \Sigma U_t^2} \qquad (2.12)$$

This equation can be rewritten somewhat more simply in (2.13).

$$a_1 = \alpha_1 + \frac{(1 - \alpha_1) [\Sigma x_t U_t + \Sigma U_t^2]}{\Sigma x_t^2 + 2 \Sigma x_t U_t + \Sigma U_t^2} \qquad (2.13)$$

Equation (2.13) allows several observations to be made. First, the expected value of a_1 is not in this case equal to α_1.[g] Thus the OLS estimator is biased. Secondly, the variance of the OLS estimator is not conveniently expressed. If k_1 is assumed to equal the expected value of the second term in (2.13), then the variance may be written:

$$\text{Var}\,(a_1) = E\,[(a_1 - \alpha_1 - k_1)^2] =$$

$$E\left[\left(\frac{(1 - \alpha_1) [\Sigma x_t U_t + \Sigma U_t^2]}{\Sigma x_t^2 + \Sigma x_t U_t + \Sigma U_t^2} - k_1\right)^2\right] \qquad (2.14)$$

Takeuchi [167] has provided a somewhat simpler expression for variance of a_1 in a similar model. However, our point is merely that the results of analytical studies (as well as those of Monte Carlo experiments) are sensitive to the assumptions made in their derivation.

One final point can be made with this case. The distribution of a_1 is now unclear. Equation (2.13) shows a_1 to be a nonlinear function of U_t, so that the assumption of normality for U_t does *not* help us in this situation.

This example illustrates the general "tactics" or the logical approach embodied in an analytical derivation of an estimator's characteristics. The process for our simple model does not seem overly difficult, which in part explains the popularity of the general linear model. However, the problems rapidly compound

---

[g]This result should not be particularly surprising. Our model is no more than a simplified version of the Haavelmo [59] case.

with simultaneous equation estimators and models. If we select models which are more representative of those used in practice, then our task is even more difficult. In the next section we shall illustrate the derivation of estimator properties with 2SLS for the same model.

The importance of this research, both exact analytical work and Monte Carlo studies, to statistical inference in econometrics cannot be overemphasized. The probability statements necessary for hypothesis testing and estimation require some knowledge of the moments of the estimators. Chebyschev's inequality applies to any random variable, but it does not require that its expectation and variance exist and are known.[h]

2.2 The Two-Stage Least Squares Estimator in a Simple Model

The results of the previous section indicate that OLS provides a biased estimator of α_1 when Equation (2.1) and (2.10) constitute the model explaining the relationship between Y_{1t}, Y_{2t}, and x_t. Two-stage least squares (hereafter 2SLS) is one member of the family of single-equation simultaneous estimators. The task of deriving the first two moments for 2SLS with this model is somewhat more difficult than with OLS.[6] First, the unrestricted least-squares estimate of the reduced form coefficient $1/1 - \alpha_1$, which shall be designated π_1, is given in (2.15).

$$\pi_1 = \frac{\Sigma Y_{2t} x_t}{\Sigma x_t^2} \tag{2.15}$$

Since the 2SLS estimator calls for the replacement of the right-hand side endogenous variable regressors by the predictions from the unrestricted reduced form, we will derive an expression for it in several steps. Equation (2.16a) expresses the relationship for the predictions from the unrestricted reduced form estimates (i.e., $\hat{Y}_{2t}$).

$$\hat{Y}_{2t} = x_t \cdot \pi_1 = x_t \cdot \frac{\Sigma Y_{2t} x_t}{\Sigma x_t^2} \tag{2.16a}$$

The 2SLS estimator of α_1 is given in (2.16b).

---

[h]This theorem allows us to state for a random variable Z with expectation r and variance σ^2 that for a positive number β. Prob $[|Z - r| \geqslant \beta] \leqslant \sigma^2/\beta^2$. That is the probability that Z will differ from r by at least β is less than σ^2/β^2. See Brunk [14] pp. 126–128.

$$\bar{a}_1 = \frac{\Sigma\, Y_{1t}\, \hat{Y}_{2t}}{\Sigma\, \hat{Y}_{2t}^{\,2}} \tag{2.16b}$$

where

$$\bar{a}_1 \;=\; \text{2SLS estimator of } \alpha_1$$

Accordingly, we can replace $\hat{Y}_{2t}$ in (2.16b) with the expression for it from (2.16a) and derive the 2SLS estimate of α_1 as follows:

$$\bar{a}_1 = \frac{\Sigma\, Y_{1t}\!\left(x_t \cdot \dfrac{\Sigma\, Y_{2t}\, x_t}{\Sigma\, x_t^{\,2}}\right)}{\Sigma\!\left(x_t \cdot \dfrac{\Sigma\, Y_{2t}\, x_t}{\Sigma\, x_t^{\,2}}\right)^{2}} = \frac{\Sigma\, Y_{1t}\, x_t}{\Sigma\, Y_{2t}\, x_t} \tag{2.16c}$$

Substituting from (2.11a) and (2.11b) for Y_{1t} and Y_{2t} into (2.16c), we can express $\bar{a}_1$ as a function of $\alpha_1, x_t,$ and U_t.

$$\bar{a}_1 = \frac{\alpha_1 \Sigma\, x_t^{\,2} + \Sigma\, x_t\, U_t}{\Sigma\, x_t^{\,2} + \Sigma\, x_t\, U_t} \tag{2.17a}$$

Or written as (2.17b)

$$\bar{a}_1 = \alpha_1 + \frac{(1 - \alpha_1) \Sigma\, x_t\, U_t}{\Sigma\, x_t^{\,2} + \Sigma\, x_t\, U_t} \tag{2.17b}$$

Since α_1 is a parameter, we can learn the nature of the moments of $\bar{a}_1$ or some linear function of $\bar{a}_1$. Thus (2.17b) can be rewritten as (2.18).

$$\frac{\bar{a}_1 - \alpha_1}{1 - \alpha_1} = \frac{b}{1 + b} \tag{2.18}$$

where

$$b = \frac{\Sigma\, x_t\, U_t}{\Sigma\, x_t^{\,2}}$$

If we assume that U_t is normally distributed with expectation of zero and variance of σ^2, then by the nature of x_t and our previous results we know that b

is normally distributed with mean zero and variance $\sigma^2/\Sigma\, x_t^2$. Accordingly, we can find the expected value of some function of b as in (2.19).

$$E\left(\frac{\bar{a}_1 - \alpha_1}{(1 - \alpha_1)}\right) = E\left(\frac{b}{1 + b}\right) =$$

$$\sqrt{\frac{1}{\dfrac{2\pi\,\sigma^2}{\Sigma\, x_t^2}}} \int_{-\infty}^{+\infty} \frac{b}{1+b} \; \exp\left(-\frac{b^2}{\dfrac{2\sigma^2}{\Sigma\, x_t^2}}\right) db \qquad (2.19)$$

However, this expression (i.e., the integral) is not defined for any finite sample. Consequently, $\bar{a}_1$'s distribution has no finite moments. This result holds even though the 2SLS estimator of α_1 is consistent.[7]

Since this conclusion is not atypical, it deserves some further explanation. What does it mean to say that the distribution of the 2SLS estimator of α_1 has no finite moments? Johnston [69] may have confused this issue in his discussion of Basmann's similar findings (with an alternative model). He notes:

Basmann has recently pointed out that it is meaningless to seek information about the bias and/or mean square deviation of an estimator if that estimator does not possess finite first or second moments. It is still, of course, meaningful to compare the frequency distributions of estimates yielded by different methods, and comparisons between sample mean square deviations for different estimators still provide some useful summary information . . .[8]

It is not really clear just what Johnston means in these statements. It is surely absurd to estimate quantities which do not exist. On the other hand, we must seek descriptive measures for characterizing the distributions in question. In order to do so, it is necessary to understand the implications of a distribution with no finite moments. A classic example in probability theory of this situation is the Cauchy distribution. The Cauchy density function satisfies the prerequisite conditions for legitimacy. Nonetheless, it does not have finite moments. Zehna [183] provides a rather helpful intuitive explanation of the meaning of such situations. He notes that:

Loosely speaking, we sometimes say that even though the area under the curve is unity, there is just too much area in the "tails" of the distribution (that is, to the right and to the left of extreme values) for the integral (expected value) . . . to converge.[9]

Thus, one heuristic conceptualization of these distributions without finite moments is that they have extremely thick tails. Nonetheless, there is still the potential for discrimination. It can be shown that once we define a standardized Cauchy density, then linear functions of it have a Cauchy distribution. Moreover, we can characterize them using a location parameter and a spread parameter.[10]

For example, let V be a standardized Cauchy distribution (i.e., $f(V) = (1/\pi)(1/1 + V^2)$, where $f(V)$ = density function), then if W is defined as in Equation (2.20) it has a Cauchy distribution. Moreover, the location parameter for W is θ and the spread parameter is λ.

$$W = \lambda V + \theta \qquad\qquad (2.20)$$

Thus, the distribution of W is centered at θ. It is also symmetric about θ.

Accordingly, we can say something more about distributions without finite moments. The problem which must be faced is the definition of a norm or a frame of reference which allows intrafamily distributional comparisons.[i] In the case of the Cauchy distribution, a standardized form was defined and the use of location and spread parameters permits such comparisons. As we shall see in the next section, there is not yet sufficient information available to begin this job with the exact finite distributions of the simultaneous equations estimators.

2.3 A Brief Review of the Exact Sampling Studies

The previous sections of this chapter have illustrated the logic underlying exact finite sample derivations in greatly simplified cases. The first step is to specify a model (as in (2.1) and (2.10)). Then it is necessary to classify the components in the model into stochastic (Y_{1t}, Y_{2t}, U_t) and nonstochastic (α_1, x_t). The stochastic elements are assumed to follow preassigned probability distributions. Given these assumptions, and the model, we attempt to derive the distributions of the components of the estimator and thereby derive the distribution of the estimated parameter. However, it is not always possible to accomplish the last two steps.

Christ [17] provides a convenient summary of the logic underlying Basmann's [7,8] work. He notes that an important assumption of the model is that all variables are exogenous. The sample mean of each variable is zero, the exogenous variables are uncorrelated in the sample, and they are measured in units which vary with the sample size.[11] Most of the density functions he and others have derived for the 2SLS (two-stage least squares) estimator have been infinite series. Consequently, if the first-order absolute moment of the estimated coefficient is to exist, each term-by-term integral must be finite.

The results of these analytical studies are dependent upon the nature of the models studies. Rather than review each author's procedures, we summarize in

---

[i]This statement makes the optimistic assumption that such a definition will in fact be possible. At this point we can only conjecture.

Table 2.1 the results of most of the exact, finite sample-studies of the simultaneous equations estimators.[j]

Several points should be emphasized with these studies. First, Basmann [8] has conjectured, and his and other results seem to support the contention, that the 2SLS estimator of the parameters of a given structural equation has finite small-sample moments up to the order of the degree of overidentification of the equation. Accordingly, if the equation is exactly identified, we might expect that no finite small sample moments exist. This case is what our example of the previous section would indicate as well. Secondly, there may be merit in exploring direct methods for deriving sample moments as Takeuchi [167] has done, rather than in working through the derivation of exact finite sample density functions. Finally, the Mariano and Sawa [104] paper indicated that the limited-information maximum-likelihood estimator of a single equation in a simultaneous system, under a fairly general model, does not possess moments of any order. This result may explain the erratic behavior found for this estimator in Monte Carlo experiments.[k]

2.4 Approximations of the Estimator's Properties

Two types of approximations used to derive the estimator properties will be briefly reviewed. The first of these is a scheme introduced by Nagar [115] [116] in which the formula for the estimator, the k-class in this case, is expanded as a series of terms of differing orders of approximation. Then the first and second moments of the estimator are derived, subject of course to the preassigned order of approximation.[12] In order to understand the approach, consider an example. Suppose that we can write an estimator of α_1, designated $\hat{a}_1$ as in Equation (2.21). While it is not necessary to provide a detailed description of each term, assume that A is a nonstochastic term, B has stochastic components, and so does D

$$\hat{a}_1 = \alpha_1 + (1 + AB)^{-1} AD \tag{2.21}$$

We might replace $(1 + AB)^{-1}$ by a power series, examine the first few terms, and learn something of the nature of $\hat{a}_1$, subject to the extent of the remainder in the omitted terms. Equation (2.22) provides such a replacement.

---

[j]Since the details in this table are necessarily abbreviated, they may seem somewhat cryptic. Consequently, the reader is urged to consult the original references for more details. Additionally, the Mariano and Sawa [104] paper is particularly clear in its exposition of the logical argument underlying the derivation and therefore, is a good starting point.

[k]See Chapter 3, Section 4.

$$\hat{a}_1 = \alpha_1 + \sum_{i=0}^{\infty} (-1)^i (AB)^i AD \qquad\qquad (2.22)$$

While the argument underlying the approximation is intuitively appealing, it suffers from at least three major defects.[13] The estimator $\hat{a}_1$ need not possess finite small-sample moments. Given such moments do not exist, then consideration of a truncated sampling error, as the Nagar procedure would call for, does not make sense. Suppose that finite first and second moments of the $\hat{a}_1$ estimator do exist, the power series expansion may not be valid. It does *not* have a theoretical basis. Finally, if we allow that both the previous objections to the approximation are not a problem, then it is not clear that its expectation, term by term, is a valid approach for finding the expected sampling error. It is clear that Dhrymes [31] has some legitimate objections to this approximation method. The errors introduced by the failure of any of these conditions to be satisfied are not capable of being evaluated. Consequently, more research is necessary before we can form a judgment as to its validity.

A second closely related approach was recently introduced by Sargan and Mikhail [144]. These authors expand the formula for the estimator, using an infinite power series, and they use the expression to derive an expansion for the distribution function for the estimator. It appears that their approach is not subject to the first of Dhrymes' three objections to Nagar's approximation scheme. There nonetheless remains the problem of the accuracy of the approximation itself. While the authors examine its behavior in the special case where the equation to be estimated contains two endogenous variables, their findings cannot be generalized to other equations.

Accordingly, it is not possible to use such approximations as a means of assessing a single estimator's properties or its behavior relative to other techniques. The performance of the approximation schemes, themselves, must first be evaluated before they will contribute substantially to estimator evaluation.

2.5   The Analytical Approach Versus Monte Carlo

In the first chapter the analytical method was compared with a deductive logical argument, while Monte Carlo experiments were characterized as inductive arguments. A choice between the two might be made based upon this analogy. That is, if one accepts the assumptions of its argument, the deductive approach provides *the valid answer*. In contrast, the inductive scheme is capable of solely probabilistic statements. Thus, the first would seem preferable. However, this simplistic evaluation can be deceiving. We do not know that the assumptions of our arguments are all upheld. Consequently, since the validity of the deductive answer is contingent upon the given assumptions and these are not held to be

Table 2.1
Tabular Survey of Exact Sampling Studies[a]

Author	Size of Model	Assumptions	Estimating Techniques	Definitive Conclusions
Basmann (7) A	2	Four exogenous variables; exogenous variables uncorrelated, means = 0; non-zero reduced form coefficients must be a function for the number of observations; errors independent between periods and normally distributed	2SLS	Finite mean and infinite variance when coefficient of right-hand side endogenous variable (RHS) not equal to zero. Finite mean, but not finite variance when coefficient of RHS = 0
Basmann (7) B	2	Similar to (7A); 1 exogenous in system under study; coefficient of RHS = 0; attempt to estimate coefficient assuming more exogenous	2SLS	Estimator of coefficient of RHS has finite mean = 0 and finite variance
Basmann (8)	3	K exogenous; reduced form coefficients of first three exogenous equal 0 in all but one equation	2SLS	Mean squared deviations should not be used when the number of excluded pre-determined variables is equal to, or less than the number of included endogenous
Kabe (75)	2 Same as Basmann	Four exogenous variables; exogenous variables uncorrelated, means = 0; non-zero reduced form coefficients must be a function of the number of observations; errors independent between periods and normally distributed	2SLS	Finite mean and infinite variance when coefficient of right-hand side (RHS) not equal to zero. Finite mean, but not finite variance when coefficient of RHS = 0
Kabe (76)	3 Same as	K exogenous; reduced form coefficients of first three exogenous equal 0 in all but one equation	2SLS	Mean squared deviations should not be used when the number of excluded pre-determined variables is equal to, or less than the number of included endogenous
Richardson (140)	One equation of at least two-equation model	$K_1 + K_2$ exogenous variables; at least two omitted from equation; two endogenous variables; disturbance is normally distributed—zero mean constant variance;	2SLS	Number of excluded exogenous variables is a parameter in density function of coefficient for RHS endogenous variable; moments exist of order one less than

Author (ref)	Number of equations	Description	Estimator	Findings
		no lagged endogenous variables; uses non-central Wishart		number of excluded exogenous variables; bias is opposite in sign to parameter of endogenous variable; mean of estimates converges to true value when convergence parameter increases; multicollinearity in exogenous variables can distort mean of estimates
Sawa (147)	2 or more	K exogenous variables; two equations of system; endogenous variables in these two do not appear elsewhere reduced form errors bivariate normally distributed; exogenous variables orthogonal. Uses non-central Wishart distribution	OLS 2SLS	Distribution of 2SLS depends crucially upon the difference between value of structural parameter and that of the regression coefficient (P) of the disturbance terms of endogenous variables; moments of order less than $N - 1$ exist for OLS, and K for 2SLS where $N =$ number of observations; $K =$ degree of overidentification
Takeuchi (167)	One equation of at least two-equation model	Two endogenous variables; case with and without exogenous variables in equation; disturbances normally distributed with zero mean	OLS 2SLS IVE[b]	Results similar to Sawa, OLS moments up to order $N - 1$ where N is sample size; 2SLS and IVE limited by the order of degree of overidentifiability; provides a direct method for sample moments rather than from densities
Basmann, Brown, Dawer, and Schoepfle (10)	3 or more equations	Examine the coefficients of the RHS endogenous variables of one equation with 3 endogenous variables and 3 exogenous variables	2SLS	Moments for the two-stage estimators of the RHS endogenous variables' coefficients do not exist
Mariano and Sawa (104)	2 or more	Examine the coefficient of RHS endogenous variable or one equation; K_1 exogenous variables	LIML[c]	Moments for the LIML estimator do not exist, regardless of the degree of over-identifiability

[a] Reprinted with permission, correction, and additions from "A Comparative Tabular Survey of Monte Carlo and Exact Sampling Studies," *Australian Economic Papers*, Vol. 10, December 1971.

[b] IVE is the abbreviation for instrumental variable estimator.

[c] LIML is the abbreviation for limited-information, single-equation maximum-likelihood estimator.

true with perfect certainty, our answer cannot be held with perfect certainty. Thus, the point is not that one provides *the answer,* while the other cannot. Rather the issue can be defined in terms of the costs and benefits of each.[1]

The cost of an analytical examination of an estimator or of a set of estimators consists of the assumptions which must be made to make the problem tractable in a mathematical sense. That is, typically the estimating techniques have been used with large, diverse models, while analytical derivations have had to assume fairly simple frameworks for their evaluations. The benefits of such studies are the gains to our understanding of each estimator's performance individually, its performance relative to likely alternatives, and finally the effects of unfulfilled assumptions on each. Thus far, as Table 2.1 indicates, our information has generally not gone beyond more details concerning one technique. Although, Sawa [147] and Takeuchi [167] have started to move forward with estimator comparisons.

The costs of the Monte Carlo approach center upon the nature of the experiments conducted. That is, while size and overall complexity of the model is not particularly a problem, specific parameterization is.[m] One or two points in the parameter space are typically all that is taken. Consequently, the results are difficult to generalize. While it is true that any number of parameterizations *could* be selected, when we consider the number of possible combinations of parameter values (including both structural parameters and error covariance matrix), model size, sample size, and any number of other characteristics, the problem becomes intractable for a different reason. The benefits from the approach are similar to those of the analytical scheme. They allow us to examine one estimator, individually, or several under a number of conditions (usually with one parameterization of the model). Our results must be interpreted. That is, since a Monte Carlo experiment provides a sample from an estimator's exact finite-sample distribution, the evaluation of the sample data is of fundamental importance to our understanding of the information provided.

What the preceding paragraphs indicate is that: (1) both are specific—one in the range of models and assumptions it can accommodate, and the other in its parameterization of a given model; (2) both provide specific results difficult to generalize, but for different reasons; (3) neither has been able to provide even a partial picture of estimator performance under the conditions usually encountered.

Consequently, there is little means for making a clearcut choice. However, we should not have to. Both approaches provide information and we should not discard a means of improving our decision making. Rather, it is necessary to learn to use the tools efficiently. Many early Monte Carlo studies employed

---

[1]Costs refer solely to a logical point of view, and not the monetary costs of supporting several analysts versus those associated with the computer runs of a set of Monte Carlo experiments.

[m]This statement assumes that the models are all linear. Nonlinear models impose substantial problems for both approaches, which neither have faced.

models wherein analytical results could be derived.[n] This approach does not seem to be an efficient use of our resources. Monte Carlo experiments should not be run as " . . . high-speed brute force computer groping . . ."[14] experiments. They need to be coordinated with analytical work which identifies the areas where answers cannot be provided with deductive analysis. Moreover, there should be a feedback between the results of Monte Carlo studies and the questions examined in an analytical framework.

2.6 Summary

The analytical methodology requires that the estimators' properties be mathematically derived from a given model and set of assumptions. While the derivations of estimator properties in many cases are difficult to understand, the logic underlying their approach is straightforward. Accordingly, a simple model was postulated in this chapter as the medium for displaying the inherent logic of the analysis.

(1) The analytical approach requires specification of a model and enumeration of the properties of the variables of the model, including the regressors and the error terms. Finally, distributional assumptions for each must be made. In order to completely describe estimator properties with these given assumptions, the estimator of a particular parameter must be expressed in terms of the variables which have probability distributions. The nature of this relationship will determine the distribution of the technique's estimates.

(2) Examination of a simple model, similar in format to the Haavelmo [59] case, easily provides a demonstration of the biased nature of the OLS estimator of the relevant coefficient (α_1). Moreover, it is also possible to show that the distribution of the 2SLS estimates of α_1 does not possess finite moments.

(3) The implications of a distribution with no finite moments are somewhat elusive. Reference to the classical case of the Cauchy distribution provides one possible heuristic view. It is possible that the area under the density function is unity and yet the extent of the area in the "tails" of the distribution prevents the expected value or other order moments from converging.

(4) A review of the analytical results for simultaneous equation estimators indicates that several points are worthy of mention.

i.   Basmann has conjectured that the 2SLS estimator of a given structural parameter has finite small-sample moments up to the order of the degree of overidentification of the equation in question. While there is no definitive proof of this statement for all cases, all the analytical results conform to it.

i.i. There may be merit in direct methods for deriving sample moments and

---

[n]See Chapter 3, Section 4 for a summary of these studies.

further research is needed in this area, since given the moments, the distribution function can be approximated.

i.i.i. Mariano and Sawa have found in a fairly general case (though not completely so) that the limited-information maximum-likelihood estimator of a single equation in a simultaneous model does not possess moments of any order.

(5) While there are techniques for the approximation of an estimator's moments, the most serious shortcoming of all approaches is the inability to gauge the degree of error introduced by the approximation under general conditions.

(6) In comparing the analytical approach versus Monte Carlo techniques, the costs and benefits in terms of assumptions, generality, and information must be assessed before a choice between the two can be made. Clearly, it is better to have a definitive answer than not. However, there are few cases in which the assumptions of the model permit such clearcut answers. Consequently, the problem is not one of choosing an approach to estimator evaluation, but rather one of coordination and feedback between the two types of research.

Notes

1. See: Christ [17] pp. 347–358, Dhrymes [31] pp. 145–160, Dutta [36] pp. 52–193, Goldberger [54] pp. 156–201, Johnston [70] pp. 8–46, Kmenta [90] pp. 197–246, Malinvaud [102] pp. 73–102, Theil [170] pp. 101–163, and Wonnacott and Wonnacott [180] pp. 1–52.

2. For a good discussion of the nature of asymptotic distribution theory, see Theil [170] pp. 357–429.

3. See Larson [95], Brunk [14], and Mood and Graybill [110] for definitions of such moments and their relationships to the nature of the density function for a continuous random variable.

4. For a good discussion of the rationale underlying the assumption of a normal distribution for U_t see Dutta [36] pp. 135–154.

5. See: Brunk [14] pp. 228–229.

6. See: Dhrymes [31] pp. 180–183 for the derivation in a model similar to the present one and more in keeping with the Haavelmo case.

7. Dhrymes [31] p. 182.

8. Johnston [69] p. 277.

9. Zehna [183] p. 100. The term "expected value," in parentheses, has been added.

10. Thomasian [171] pp. 387–391.

11. Christ [17] pp. 472–474.

12. See: Dhrymes [31] pp. 200–208 for a discussion of the Nagar [115] approach and Theil [170] pp. 358–359 for a discussion of the order of approximation operator (i.e., big O and little o).

13. Dhrymes [31] p. 204.

14. Arnoff [5] p. 146.

3

The Monte Carlo Literature: A Representative Sampling

Sampling experiments have tended to focus attention upon intractable analytical problems which may have some important implications for applications. They have been conducted with both single and simultaneous equation models. Moreover, within each class of models a variety of problems has been addressed. The studies reviewed in this chapter have been divided into two broad categories based upon the nature of the model. Within the single equation framework, the particular problems studied allow for convenient subdivisions. Accordingly, the first section summarizes the findings with studies of autocorrelation in the general linear model and distributed lag techniques. It is followed by discussions of the work with models having nonnormal error structures and joint estimators for single equation models.

The second half of the chapter deals with the experiments performed to evaluate estimators for simultaneous equation models. These studies have been reviewed more or less chronologically, since a variety of problems were considered in each. The more recent contributions have been given more detailed attention than the early, fairly limited studies.

3.1 Single Equation Problems: Autocorrelation and Distributed Lags

In the examples used in Chapter 2 to illustrate the logic of the analytical approach to the evaluation of estimator properties, the causal relationship between dependent and independent variables was assumed to be instantaneous. That is, a change in one of the independent variables caused a change in the dependent variable within the same time period. In many cases this assumption is untenable. Consequently, the need to specify the dynamic nature of adjustment patterns has been a primary influence in the development of distributed lag models, where the results of a change in an independent variable are spread over a number of time periods.[1]

In such models, ordinary least squares and several other techniques are available for estimation. Many within this set are recommended on the basis of their asymptotic properties. As we have noted in the preceding chapters, such evaluations are not clearly relevant to situations in which the samples available are of limited size. Since it has proved difficult to derive the small-sample properties of these techniques analytically, a number of Monte Carlo studies have sought to provide an alternative source of information. In what follows, we will summarize several of the studies in this and related areas.

If we assume that the lag distribution is geometric, where the effects of some independent variable x extend indefinitely into the past, but the coefficients of their respective impacts decline in a fixed proportion, then using a "Koyck transformation" the model may be written as (3.1).

$$Y_t = \alpha Y_{t-1} + \beta x_t + U_t \qquad (3.1)$$

If the error associated with the model in its untransformed state satisfies the assumptions of the classical model (i.e., i.i.i. in (2.2) primarily), then U_t will be autocorrelated as in (3.2).

$$U_t = \lambda U_{t-1} + e_t \qquad (3.2)$$

where

e_t satisfies the assumptions of the classical model and $0 < \lambda < 1$.

This basic model was investigated by Taylor and Wilson [168] in 1964, when they proposed an estimator for the model and named it three-pass least squares (hereafter 3PLS).[a] They suggest on asymptotic grounds that 3PLS will be more desirable than OLS for this model and for the dynamic-demand model specification as well.[b] In order to examine the respective small-sample properties of each, the authors perform twenty-one experiments, most of which contain twenty-five samples (or replicates).[c] The experiments differ according to: (a) the size of each sample (i.e., 50, 30, 20 observations); (b) the degree of fit of the theoretical model measured by the coefficient of determination; (c) the character of the autocorrelation in the error including, order, direction (i.e., positive or negative), and level (i.e., high or low absolute magnitude of λ). Their primary measures of performance were mean, bias, standard deviation, and mean squared error of the estimates.

Their results generally indicate that 3PLS is superior to OLS, especially

---

[a]This technique is applied as follows: First, apply OLS to the model in (3.1), use the OLS residuals to estimate

$(Y - \hat{\beta}x)_t = \alpha_1 Y_{t-1} + \gamma \hat{U}_{t-1} + \theta Y_{t-2}$

with β = OLS estimate of β. Then, the residuals from this regression are used to estimate an equation derived by substituting in (3.1) from (3.2) for U_t. It is:

$Y_t = \alpha Y_{t-1} + \beta x_t + \lambda \hat{U}_{t-1} + \epsilon_t$.

[b]The dynamic demand model is:

$Y_t = \theta_0 + \theta_1 Y_{t-1} + \theta_2 x_t + \theta_3 x_{t-1} + \lambda U_{t-1} + \epsilon_t$

[c]The only exception to this statement is the experiment with the dynamic demand model which has 100 samples.

when there is substantial autocorrelation. The three-pass technique has a smaller bias and is more efficient. Neither estimator is appreciably affected by minor second-order effects. However, OLS is seriously affected by explosive (i.e., $|\lambda| \geqslant 1$) processes. The sample size and low levels of autocorrelation do not reduce the superiority of 3PLS over OLS. Moreover, 3PLS is marginally better than OLS for Koyck-type models. The only case in which there is some question in their ranking of these two techniques occurs with strong negative autocorrelation (i.e., $0 > \lambda > -1$). The clearest limitation with the Taylor–Wilson work is their failure to consider other techniques for estimating this model. In addition, the number of replicates within each experiment is also somewhat limited.

A partial remedy to these problems is provided by Wallis' [176] 1967 study. His work increases the number of techniques considered by two, in addition to 3PLS and OLS. The number of samples in each experiment is increased to 100. However, these advantages are somewhat offset by the smaller number of experiments—five in total.[d] The estimators added are a two-stage Aitken generalized technique and an instrumental variable estimator (hereafter GLS and IVE, respectively). Each sample contains fifty observations and the five experiments are distinguished on the basis of the magnitude of the positive autocorrelation coefficient and the degree of fit of the theoretical relationship.

Wallis first subjects three approaches to the estimation of the autocorrelation coefficient (λ) to evaluation before proceeding to examine the specific problem. This choice between a minimum chi square, least squares, and first-order serial correlation coefficient is an important determinant of the properties of the GLS estimator.[2] The best overall performance was given by the first-order serial correlation coefficient with a correction for bias. Consequently, it was estimated from the residuals of an instrumental variable estimate of (3.1), with x_{t-1} as an instrument for Y_{t-1} and then used in the GLS estimation.

The mean, bias, standard deviation, and mean squared error of the estimates were used to evaluate each technique. In addition, the mean absolute errors of GLS and 3PLS are presented. Finally, the number of samples, in a given experiment, in which the GLS estimate is closer to the true value than the 3PLS estimate is tested to determine whether or not it is significantly different from fifty. Overall, using all criteria, Wallis found that GLS is superior to 3PLS. This Aitken estimator is found to be more efficient than 3PLS.

In a 1968 paper, Sargent [145] further expanded the number of estimators to include not only OLS and 3PLS, but also Leviatan's instrumental variable estimator (hereafter LIVE), an errors in variables estimator (hereafter EVE),[3] Klein's maximum likelihood technique (hereafter KML),[4] and an iterative technique (hereafter SIT) which iterates on the serial correlation coefficient, estimating it simultaneously with the other parameters using OLS residuals, the first round residuals, and previous solutions' residuals thereafter.

---

[d]These comments are not criticisms of the results, but merely comments on the design of the research.

Sargent performs twelve experiments. Each experiment contains twenty-five samples or replicates in which each has thirty-five observations. Alteration in α, β, and λ in Equations (3.1) and (3.2), as well as the scheme for generating the errors, distinguishes his experiments. The evaluation criteria include bias, mean squared error, and the mean absolute deviation of the estimates for α, β, and λ.

His results indicate that the more sophisticated techniques adjust the bias in measurement of α toward zero. However, this conclusion should be qualified to reflect the fact that the relative performance of all techniques is sensitive to the parameterization of the model. This sensitivity is particularly apparent with LIVE and 3PLS. KML and SIT are not as subject to it.

Since the efficiency of each technique depends upon the disturbance variance, and the Koyck transformation alters it, then the best form for estimating the model will depend critically on the error scheme. Another important aspect of Sargent's results indicates that either 3PLS or SIT may be better indicators of positive autocorrelation than the Durbin–Watson test. Finally, if one uses the mean absolute deviation criterion, 3PLS is best followed by SIT. Perhaps the most important finding of Sargent's work is that the results are not as clearcut as the previous two studies would lead us to believe. The techniques are indeed sensitive to the environment within which they are evaluated. Moreover, under different objective or loss functions, our choices will change.

In a somewhat less general model, Thornber [172] raises a number of fundamental questions relating to the general role of Monte Carlo experiments, and more specifically the design of such research, so as to support and complement analytical results. Equation (3.3) presents his basic model.

$$Y_t = \theta Y_{t-1} + v_t \tag{3.3}$$

Four estimators for this model are considered including OLS, weighted least squares (hereafter WLS), maximum likelihood technique (ML), and a Bayesian approach (BE).[e] Ten different experiments distinguished by the size of θ, each with 100 samples of 20 observations are performed so that the risk functions for each technique may be estimated. That is, the risk function which defines the average loss (in terms of mean squared error) as a function of θ is estimated with

---

[e]The first three techniques are given as follows:

$$\theta_{OLS} = \frac{\Sigma Y_t Y_{t-1}}{\Sigma Y_{t-1}^2}$$

$$\theta_{WLS} = \frac{\Sigma Y_t Y_{t-1}}{\Sigma Y_{t-1}^2 - Y_0^2}$$

the ten observations, each derived from the experiments. The risk functions were postulated as quadratic in θ, and were fitted using a weighted least-squares procedure, where the weights were the reciprocals of the observed within-group variance for each θ.

While the Thornber paper's primary contribution is in its commentary upon Monte Carlo methodology, his experiments do indicate that the Bayesian technique is best, a constrained estimator (i.e., if OLS estimate of $\theta > 1$, set $\theta = 1$) is second best, and OLS is the third choice.

Using a similar model, Orcutt and Winokur [126] study the performance of OLS in an autoregressive model.[f] Ten thousand replicates in each of three experiments were performed to investigate the joint frequency distribution of estimates of the constant term and of the slope. The experiments are distinguished by the value for the slope. The sample size was kept at ten observations. These experiments indicate that joint hypothesis testing cannot use the F and Student-t distributions. The underlying assumption of joint normality appears to be violated in the model.

In a further set of forty-eight experiments, each with one-thousand trials, the authors investigate the estimates of the slope coefficient and error variance. The experiments are distinguished on the basis of the true values of the slope and the sample size. The results indicate that the Student-t distribution can be used for inference about the level of a first-order autogressive process, and equally important, a chi square distribution may be used for inference with the residual error variance. Evaluation of the efficiency of least-squares prediction indicates that it is nearly optimal in small samples.

One fine example of a carefully designed sequence of experiments and a useful summary of their results is provided in a paper by Rao and Griliches [138]. The authors perform 200 experiments each with 50 samples of 20 observations. Their objective is to assess the efficiency of alternative two-stage estimators of a linear regression model with first-order correlation. The techniques include in addition to OLS, the Cochrane–Orcutt (CO) approach, Durbin's

---

θ_{ML} = root of the following expression

$$\theta^3 + \frac{(T-2)}{(T-1)} \cdot \frac{M_1}{2M_1} \theta^2 - \frac{M_0 + TM_2}{M_2(T-1)} \theta - \frac{(T-1)}{T} \frac{M_1}{2M_2} = 0$$

where T = sample size

$M_0 = \Sigma Y_t^2$
$M_1 = -2 \Sigma Y_t Y_{t-1}$
$M_2 = \Sigma Y_{t-1}^2$

The Bayesian estimator is derived under a minimum expected loss criteria using a quadratic loss function. See Thornber [172] pp. 804–806.

[f]Actually the Orcutt-Winokur model contains an intercept and a slope coefficient.

method (DM), the Prais–Winsten technique (PW), and a nonlinear maximum likelihood approach (NT).[g]

The Rao–Griliches' model is given in Equation (3.4)

$$Y_t = \beta x_t + U_t$$

$$x_t = \lambda x_{t-1} + v_t$$

$$U_t = \theta U_{t-1} + w_t \qquad\qquad (3.4)$$

where

v_t, w_t are independent random variables which are not autocorrelated.

$|\lambda| < 1$

$|\theta| < 1$

The two hundred experiments are distinguished by the pair of values for λ and θ. Twenty values of θ are selected in one-tenth intervals from minus one to plus one, and ten for λ in two-tenths intervals over the same range.

The bias and mean squared error are presented for each technique. The estimates of θ indicate that the Durbin approach is better than OLS or the nonlinear technique when θ is a high positive value, and the NT approach is better for large negative values. In the middle range neither is appreciably better than OLS.[h] When the techniques are compared for their performance estimating β, the results indicate that the OLS approach is best for low and moderate absolute values of θ. None of the other estimators have appreciably different performance patterns with this coefficient. The NT approach seems somewhat inferior to the two-stage approaches. The Rao–Griliches results also indicate that:

For small values of θ efficiency of the O.L.S. estimator of β is quite high and increases with the autocorrelation of the independent variable.[5]

Consequently, certain loss functions may suggest that it is unnecessary to perform the adjustments implied by the other techniques.

---

[g]The Cochrane–Orcutt approach replaces each value of the dependent and independent variables by $Z_{it} - \hat{\theta} Z_{it-1}$, where Z_t is the tth observation on the variable and $\hat{\theta}$ is a consistent estimate of the autocorrelation. The Durbin method is similar, but estimates θ differently. The Prais–Winsten approach is the Aitken estimator using a consistent estimate of θ. Finally the nonlinear estimator estimates $Y_1 = \theta Y_{t-1} + \beta x_t - \beta \theta x_{t-1} + U_t$, subject to $\beta \theta = \hat{\theta} \cdot \hat{\beta}$, by minimizing the sum of squared residuals.

[h]The nonlinear approach is conceptually similar to the Dhrymes iterative approach discussed in what follows.

Overall, their findings indicate that the DM for estimating θ, used in conjunction with the PW adjustment scheme, is likely to be better over a wider range of parameter values than the other approaches.

The remaining three studies summarized in this section compare estimators of distributed lag models in their transformed format, similar to (3.1), relative to those of the untransformed model given in (3.5).

$$Y_t = \gamma \sum_{i=0}^{\infty} \lambda^i x_{t-i} + w_t \qquad (3.5)$$

where:

w_t is classically well behaved.

The first of these is a paper by Morrison [112]. His experiments, some twelve in total, consider OLS, EVE, LIVE, an iterative scheme developed by Steiglitz and McBride (ISM), Dhrymes iterative estimator (DIE), and Hannan's spectral estimates (HSE).[i] Each experiment contains fifty samples. The features which distinguish them are: sample size, relative size of the stochastic component's variation to the total of the model, and the value of λ.

With small values of λ and a low variance ratio, OLS performs reasonably well. In fact, it may be preferable to LIVE under favorable conditions. This conclusion is not clearcut since the EVE technique, OLS, and LIVE are approximately equivalent for low λ, variance ratio, and small samples. The primary criteria used in this evaluation are the mean of the sample estimates and the root mean squared error. Over all, considering variations in λ, sample size (20 versus 50), and large versus small variance ratios, the ISM technique is found to be best with DIE a close second.

Schmidt's [150] 1971 paper considers the same model as that of Morrison, with one important exception regarding the error properties. w_t in Equation (3.5) is assumed to follow a second order autoregressive process as in (3.6).

---

[i]The techniques not previously discussed and defined are the iterative approach of Steiglitz and McBride, Dhrymes' iterative approach, and Hannan's spectral estimates. The first of these uses Klein's maximum likelihood equation (see Klein [82], Morrison 112]), uses initial consistent estimates of γ and λ to linearize the equations, so estimates of these parameters may be used for "prefiltering" the data before the next solution. The Dhrymes approach iterates on λ solving for the γ and

$$\sum_{i=t}^{\infty} \lambda^{i-t} x_{t-i}$$

which minimize the sum of squared errors. Finally, the Hannan equations were derived from a frequency domain model which can be approximately converted to an Aitken estimator. See Amemiya and Fuller [4], Hannan [64].

$$w_t = \delta_1 w_{t-1} + \delta_2 w_{t-2} + v_t \tag{3.6}$$

where

v_t is well behaved.

Schmidt's objective is to evaluate Dhrymes' iterative maximum likelihood estimator (DIE) under a variety of conditions, including variations in the order of the autocorrelation in w_t, sample size, and magnitude of δ_1 and δ_2. It should be noted that the autocorrelation referred to with the Morrison model resulted from transformation of a model with a well behaved w_t to a format corresponding to (3.1). In this case w_t is *not* well-behaved and transformation (if $\lambda \neq \delta_1$) will merely convolute the error structure. This distinction is most important in evaluating the results of the two studies in a comparative sense. Only in the case where both δ_1 and δ_2 are zero in the Schmidt scheme, will there be some conformance with Morrison's work.

Schmidt performs a total of seventeen experiments. Samples of size 50 and 100 are repeated fifty times in these experiments and those of 20 are repeated one-hundred times. The mean, variance, and mean squared error of the estimates are presented for evaluation. The most important finding is that the asymptotic properties of DIE seem to be a good guide to the small-sample properties even with samples of size 20. Understating the order of autocorrelation leads to "bad" performance for DIE, while an overstatement of the order (e.g., second order when actually first order) seems to be costless in its effects upon the estimator.

In his recent comprehensive book on distributed lag models, Dhrymes [33] reports the results of a series of Monte Carlo studies with the model of (3.5) and with a model similar to (3.1). The error structure of w_t is assumed to follow a first-order autoregressive pattern. Forty-five experiments each with one-hundred replications are performed. They may be distinguished by the sample size (20, 50, 100), the magnitude of λ, and the magnitude of the autocorrelation coefficient (i.e., δ_1 in (3.5), since $\delta_2 = 0$). The bias and mean squared error of the estimates are used to evaluate the performance of DIE. In general, Dhrymes' results conform to those of Schmidt. DIE has relatively small bias and mean squared error with small samples. In addition, the bias in estimation of λ declines as the true value diminishes.

The second set of experiments relates to the model given in (3.1) with a first order autoregressive error. Some eighty-eight experiments differentiated on the basis of sample size (i.e., 10, 20, 40, 80, 160, 320, 640, 1280), values of α, and of λ, in (3.2) were performed to evaluate OLS, a maximum likelihood estimator (ML), a minimum chi-square technique (MCS), and an Aitken estimator where OLS estimates of λ are used in constructing the error covariance structure (GLSI).[j]

---

[j]The residuals used to estimate λ are from instrumental variable estimation of (3.1) with x_{t-1} as instrument for Y_{t-1}. See Dhrymes [33] pp. 370–374 for details.

In general ML dominates the other techniques. However, the performance patterns of ML and MCS, using bias and mean squared error, are quite similar. The GLSI approach exhibits comparable performance only when the ratio of the variance in the random components to systematic is small. Finally, asymptotic moments provide a fairly good guide to the small sample estimates even for samples of approximately forty observations.

Table 3.1 summarizes the key attributes of each of the aforementioned studies. While the performance patterns of the techniques evaluated are quite sensitive to the parameters of the model, 3PLS, GLS, and DIE seem to be the most robust of the techniques evaluated. Though comparisons across Monte Carlo studies are difficult and hazardous because of the differences in design features, it is probably safe to say that a set of techniques including 3PLS, GLS, DIE, LIVE, and ISM is fairly comparable in performance patterns. All these techniques have somewhat comparable asymptotic characteristics as well as small sample properties.

3.2 Single Equation Problems:
Parent Distribution of Error

Recent works by Zeckhauser and Thompson [182] and Fama [42] have questioned the assumption of normality of error terms which is characteristically made for hypothesis testing with linear models.[6] As a consequence, there have been a limited number of studies investigating estimators for linear single equation models with nonnormal errors. Once again, the primary reason for the sampling or Monte Carlo approach stems from the intractability of the problem in analytical form.

The two studies in this area are by Blattberg and Sargent [12] and Smith and Hall [161]. In the first of these, two types of estimators, in addition to OLS, are considered in the context of a stable symmetric Paretian distribution. The first type of technique is the best linear unbiased estimator derived for models with stable Paretian distributions. Since the Gauss Markov theorem, which shows OLS to be the minimum variance estimator of the class of linear unbiased techniques, applies only in those cases where the error structure follows a distribution with a finite variance, OLS will *not* be BLUE (best linear unbiased estimator) for all members of this class. Blattberg and Sargent suggest a technique which is equivalent to OLS, when the distribution is normal and maintains the BLUE property otherwise (BLUE-P).[k] The second category is a technique which

---

[k]If the model is written as: $Y_j = B x_j + U_j$, then

$$\bar{B}(\alpha) = \frac{\sum_j |x_j|^{1/(\alpha-1)} Y_j \cdot \text{sign}(x_j)}{\sum_j |x_j|^{\alpha/(\alpha-1)}}$$

where: α = characteristic exponent. If $\alpha = 2$, then the distribution is normal and the estimator is OLS.

Table 3.1
Summary of Autocorrelation and Distributed Lag Model Results

Author	Direction and Degree of Autocorrelation	Size of Sample	Estimating Techniques Evaluated	Experimental Features	Definitive Conclusions	No. of Trials
Taylor and Wilson (168)	Positive and negative; first and minor second order	20 30 50	OLS 3PLS	21 experiments; high and low R^2 (goodness of fit); evaluates dynamic demand equations; autocorrelation coefficient ranges from -0.9 to +1.0	OLS and 3PLS are not affected by minor second order effects; OLS completely deficient with explosive process; 3PLS more efficient and smaller bias than OLS in all but strong negative autocorrelation	25
Wallis (176)	Positive and first order	50	OLS 3PLS GLS IVE	5 experiments; considers three estimators of the autocorrelation coefficient prior to their use in the GLS technique. Autocorrelation 0.5 and 0.8; varying R^2	GLS is more efficient than 3PLS in all cases	100
Sargent (145)	Positive autocorrelation	35	OLS 3PLS LIVE EVE SIT	12 experiments, autocorrelation from 0.1 to 0.9; two error generating schemes; alternative parameterizations	Estimators sensitive to parameterization; criteria of mean absolute deviation would rate 3PLS as the best	25
Thornber (172)	First order autoregressive model	20	OLS WLS ML BE	10 experiments each distinguished by value of θ; Use average loss (MSE) results to estimate quadratic risk function	Bayesian estimator derived under a minimum expected loss criteria with a quadratic loss function is best technique	100
Orcutt and Winokur (126)	First order autoregressive model	10 20 40	OLS	Two separate sets of experiments were performed. The first is used to evaluate the joint distribution of the intercept and slope -3 in all. The second set, 48 in total evaluates estimates of the slope and residual variance	t-distribution can be used for inference about the level of a first order process; chi-square for inference with residual error variance; bivariate normal cannot be used for inference about slope and level jointly	I- 10,000 II- 1,000

Study	Model	Sample sizes	Estimators	Experiments	Findings	
Rao and Griliches (138)	First order autoregressive model	20	OLS CO DM PW NT	Two hundred experiments indexed on θ and λ. Bias and mean squared error are used to evaluate estimates of θ and β	For low absolute magnitudes of efficiency of OLS estimator of θ, β is quite high. For largest range of parameter values, DM is likely to do best	50
Morrison (112)	Positive first order	20 50	OLS EVE LIVE ISM DIE HSE	Twelve experiments were conducted; each is distinguished by sample size, relative size of stochastic components variation to the total of the model, and the value of the autocorrelation coefficient	Overall, considering variations in the three factors (sample size, variance ratio, and auto-correlation), ISM is found to be the best technique with DIE a close second. For a small variance ratios and autocorrelation OLS$\approx$EVE$\approx$LIVE	50
Schmidt (150)	Positive first and second order	20 50 100	DIE	Seventeen experiments are performed. They consider no, first order and second order autocorrelation. DIE is applied under alternative assumptions concerning the "true" order of the error structure	The asymptotic properties of DIE seem to be a good guide to small sample properties. Understanding the order of autocorrelation leads to poor performance for DIE, while overstatement seems to be costless	100 for samples of 20, 50 otherwise
Dhrymes (33) A	Positive first order	20 50 100	DIE	Forty-five experiments with alteration in magnitude of λ and δ_1. Bias and mean squared error are criteria for estimator evaluation	DIE has small bias and mean squared error even with small samples. Bias in estimation of λ declines with size of λ	100
Dhrymes (33) B	Positive first order	10 20 40 80 160 320 640 1280	OLS ML MCS GLSI	Eighty-eight experiments distinguished by α and λ in (3.1) and (3.2) and sample size	ML dominates other techniques. However, GLSI is good performer when ratio of variance in error to systematic components of the model is small. Asymptotic results are a good guide to small sample properties	50

selects the estimates so as to minimize the sum of absolute deviations. This technique is the maximum likelihood estimator for models with a double-exponential or Laplace distribution and consequently may be desirable for other thick-tailed distributions such as the stable Paretian distribution.

The authors conduct six experiments each with one hundred samples of fifty observations with the model given in Equation (3.7).

$$Y_j = 3 x_j + U_j \qquad\qquad\qquad\qquad\qquad\qquad (3.7)$$

Two measures of the performance of the techniques are presented. The first is an estimator of the semi-interquartile range and the second the average absolute deviation.

The results indicate that the minimum absolute deviation (MAD) technique is superior to OLS and the BLUE technique for stable Paretian distributions when the characteristic exponent (i.e., an indicator of fatness of the tails of the distribution) is small. This superiority will also hold for nonstable distributions. While some of these other distributons have finite variances, they are denser over portions of the extreme tails of the distributions than that exhibited by the normal distribution.

The Smith–Hall [161] study considers one member of the thick-tailed distributions whose error variance exists. This one is the double exponential. Nine experiments, each with fifty samples of twenty observations were performed to compare the OLS and MAD techniques. They can be broken down by two criteria: (1) the model used for data generation and (2) the size of the variance in the error terms. Two models with two regressors distinguished by the collinearity in the regressors and one with three regressors are the structures used.

The mean, root mean squared error, bias, and variance in the estimates are reported. In addition, Kendall's coefficient of concordance was applied to examine the consistency in the ranking (according to absolute bias) of the two techniques across the trials. The results reinforce the findings of Blattberg and Sargent and support the use of MAD.[7] Moreover, it appears that OLS is more sensitive to multicollinearity than MAD.

Table 3.2 summarizes the salient features of these two studies. Perhaps their greatest limitations lie in the range of models, error distributions, and estimators considered. For one thing, the MAD technique, which seems to be the desired approach, does not provide a readily derivable covariance structure. Consequently, we cannot gauge the error in our estimates in a manner comparable to OLS. Further research will need to focus attention upon these problems.

3.3 Seemingly Unrelated Regressions: Small Sample Results

The properties derived for OLS in estimating the classical linear model are contingent upon the fulfillment of the assumptions of the model. In the previous

Table 3.2
Summary of Monte Carlo Studies for Parent Distribution of Error Problems

Author	Error Distribution	Size of Sample	Estimating Techniques Evaluated	Experimental Features	Definitive Conclusions	No. of Trials
Blattberg and Sargent (12)	Stable Paretian	50	OLS MAD BLUE-P	Six experiments each with different extent of "thickness" in the tails of the distribution (as measured by the characteristic exponent)	MAD is superior to OLS and BLUE-P when "thickness" of the tails of the distribution is great	100
Smith and Hall (161)	Double Exponential	20	OLS MAD	Nine experiments designed so as to compare BLUE property with maximum likelihood. Multicollinearity and error variance also considered	MAD is superior to OLS; moreover it is less sensitive to collinearity than OLS	50

two sections we have noted that alteration in the form of the model may result in unsatisfied assumptions and consequently, there remains scope for alternative estimators.

In addition to the assumptions stated in Chapter 2, there is also an implicit assumption made that we are using all available information. If there exists other information, such as joint movement between the errors in the equation of interest and errors associated with another equation, then the results for OLS cannot be considered as proven.[8] The seemingly unrelated regressions estimator was first introduced by Zellner [184] and has been extensively used since that time.[9] The basic idea underlying the technique consists in arraying the data matrices for the equations in question so that the contemporaneous covariances between their errors may be used in an Aitken estimator of the parameters.

Consider the following two-equation example:

$$Y_1 = x_1 \beta_1 + U_1 \tag{3.8a}$$

$$Y_2 = x_2 \beta_2 + U_2 \tag{3.8b}$$

where:

Y_1, Y_2 are Tx1 vectors of observations on the dependent variables.

x_1, x_2 are Tx1 vectors of observations on the two regressors.[1]

U_1, U_2 are Tx1 vectors of observations on the two errors.

We are assuming that the contemporaneous covariance of the errors is not zero (i.e., Cov $(U_{1t}, U_{2t}) \neq 0$). Rewriting (3.8a) and (3.8b) in matrix form results in (3.9).

$$\begin{bmatrix} Y_1 \\ Y_2 \end{bmatrix} = \begin{bmatrix} x_1 & 0 \\ 0 & x_2 \end{bmatrix} \begin{bmatrix} \beta_1 \\ \beta_2 \end{bmatrix} + \begin{bmatrix} U_1 \\ U_2 \end{bmatrix} \tag{3.9}$$

or

$$Y = x \beta + U \tag{3.9a}$$

The Aitken estimator for the parameters of this general statement (i.e., 3.9a) is given in (3.9b). It should be noted that estimation requires knowledge of the

---

[1]Note that there can be more than one regressor in each set; they need not have an equal number in the two equations and if they are identical in both equations, the seemingly unrelated regressions technique reduces to OLS.

population covariance matrix of U. The alternative estimators for these models may be distinguished according to their approaches to the estimation of this error structure.[10]

$$\beta = (x^T \Sigma^{-1} x)^{-1} (x^T \Sigma^{-1} Y) \tag{3.9b}$$

where:

$$\Sigma = \begin{bmatrix} \text{Var}(U_1) & \text{Cov}(U_1 \ U_2) \\ \text{Cov}(U_1 \ U_2) & \text{Var}(U_2) \end{bmatrix} \circledX \quad I \tag{3.9b}$$

Kmenta and Gilbert [91], [92] have provided some fairly detailed information on the small sample properties of alternative estimators for this model under a variety of conditions. In their first study in 1968, they examine five estimators for the model including OLS; an Aitken procedure which uses the OLS residuals to estimate Σ (designated ZEF); Telser's [169] iterative estimator (designated TIE)[11]; Zellner's iterative approach (designated IZEF), which uses the ZEF scheme to obtain residuals and reestimate Σ, and continues until the parameter estimates converge; and finally, a maximum-likelihood approach, under the assumption that the errors are normally distributed (ML).

The authors perform forty-eight experiments, each with one hundred replicates. The factors which distinguish the experiments are: sample size (10, 20, 100), model size, correlation in the regressors, and error structure. Nine error structures are used with subsets of the four possible models. Model 1 is a two-equation model with two regressors in each equation. The four regressors are *not* highly correlated. The second model repeats the same structure with highly correlated regressors. Model 3 contains four equations, each with two regressors (having moderate correlations). The last model is a two-equation structure in which lagged endogenous variables are included in the regressors of each equation.

There were nine error structures studied including: highly correlated disturbances (A), moderate correlation (B), differential variance size and moderate correlation (C), uncorrelated (D), heteroscedastic disturbances (E and F), and finally, first order autoregressive errors with strongly linked errors across equations (G), moderately linked (H) and independent (I). Table 3.3 summarizes how the models were linked with the error structures. Each pair (model and error structure) was used with the three sample sizes.

The evaluation of the techniques is based upon the mean and standard deviations of the estimates. The first result of some importance is that TIE, IZEF, and ML led to *identical* results in every sample. In addition, all the estimators are unbiased in most of the cases considered. ZEF is superior to OLS except when the errors are not correlated. Moreover, ZEF's performance is

Table 3.3
Kmenta and Gilbert Experiments with the Seemingly Unrelated
Regressions Estimator

Error Structure	Model			
	1	2	3	4
A	(1, A)	(2, A)	(3, A)	(4, A)
B	(1, B)	(2, B)	(3, B)	(4, B)
C	(1, C)			
D	(1, D)			
E	(1, E)			
F	(1, F)			
G	(1, G)	(2, G)		
H	(1, H)			
I	(1, I)			

consistently better under all the misspecifications of the assumptions of the model considered in the experiments.

In all cases except ((1, A),(1, G) and (1, H)) ZEF has a smaller variance than ML. It appears, on the basis of the Kmenta–Gilbert results, that some efficiency may be lost by using iterative over two-stage Aitken estimators.

The second Monte Carlo study with the seemingly unrelated regressions estimator examines their properties when we attempt to account for autoregressive processes which may be present. Six estimators are considered in these experiments including OLS, ZEF, a three stage Aitken procedure (ZEF-OLS) proposed by Parks [127] which calls for estimating the autocorrelation coefficients for each equation from the OLS residuals, a four stage approach which estimates the autocorrelation using ZEF residuals (ZEF-ZEF), estimation of the autocorrelation using nonlinear least squares for each equation and then perform the seemingly unrelated regressions with the transformed data, and finally a procedure which minimizes the "system error" and jointly estimates the parameters and autocorrelation coefficients for the system (ZEF-OLNEST and JOINTEST, respectively).[12]

Three models with each of three sample sizes (10, 20, 100) constitute the experiments used to evaluate these techniques. Each experiment contains one hundred samples and the models are distinguished on the basis of the degree of correlation across the equations. All of the preceding techniques are unbiased, so the results reported by the authors consist of the standard deviations of the estimates. On the basis of these results ZEF is superior to OLS and, equally important, all of the other four techniques are better than ZEF.

Kmenta and Gilbert use the number of times the standard deviation of the coefficient estimates was less than the median of the four remaining rechniques as a criterion for ranking them. The results indicate that, with a maximum of twelve, JOINTEST is better eleven times, ZEF–ZEF eight, ZEF–OLNEST four, and ZEF–OLS once.[m] An important general finding indicates that:

> . . . whatever the size of the sample, the estimation methods which allow for both types of correlation lead to more efficient estimates of the regression coefficients than other methods.[13]

While the models are completely different, this finding is consistent with that of Schmidt [150] in his examination of the DIE (Dhrymes iterative maximum likelihood) estimator for distributed lag models. That is, with time series data, whether we are using a single equation technique or a system estimator, our results are likely to be better if we assume autocorrelation is present and select estimators to account for it.

3.4 Simultaneous Equation Estimators: Part I[n]

As the introduction to this chapter noted, the Monte Carlo research investigating the small sample properties of estimators for linear simultaneous equation models will be partitioned into four segments. This first component will deal with the early work in the area including Summers' [166] study. It will be followed by separate sections considering individually the work of Cragg [24], [25], [26], [27], Mosbaek and Wold [113], Sasser [146], and Goldfeld and Quandt [57].

Over fifteen years ago, George Ladd [94] performed a sampling experiment to investigate the properties of ordinary least squares (henceforth designated DLS, for direct least-squares, to distinguish it from ordinary least-squares on the reduced form) and limited information single-equation (LISE) in the presence of measurement errors. The model used to investigate the properties of the techniques is given in (3.10) below. It is a two equation, overidentified model where four of the predetermined variables are exogenous.

$$
\begin{bmatrix} -1 & \beta_{12} \\ -1 & \beta_{22} \end{bmatrix}
\begin{bmatrix} Y_{1t} \\ Y_{2t} \end{bmatrix}
+
\begin{bmatrix} \gamma_{10} & \gamma_{11} & \gamma_{12} & 0 & 0 \\ \gamma_{20} & 0 & 0 & \gamma_{23} & \gamma_{24} \end{bmatrix}
\begin{bmatrix} 1 \\ Z_{1t} \\ Z_{2t} \\ Z_{3t} \\ Z_{4t} \end{bmatrix}
+
\begin{bmatrix} U_{1t} \\ U_{2t} \end{bmatrix}
= 0
\qquad (3.10)
$$

[m]The number twelve was determined by the fact that the model used in the study was a two-equation model. Each equation contained one regressor and an intercept. Looking at the coefficients of the two regressors for three models with the two small samples, we have twelve possibilities.

[n]See Appendix C for a brief discussion of the econometric estimators.

where

Y_{it} = endogenous variable

Z_{it} = predetermined variable

U_{it} = random disturbance

His experiment includes thirty samples, each with thirty observations and his findings indicate that DLS exhibits a greater bias, but smaller standard deviation of the estimates, than LISE

Wagner [184] two years later, investigated the performance of these two techniques and an instrumental variable estimator (IVE) with a three-equation model. One of the equations was postulated to be an identity which was substituted into the second equation before estimation. The model, in matrix form, is given in (3.11).

$$\begin{bmatrix} 1 & -\beta_1 \\ -1 & 1-\beta_2 \end{bmatrix} \begin{bmatrix} Y_{1t} \\ Y_{2t} \end{bmatrix} + \begin{bmatrix} -\gamma_1 & 0 & 0 \\ -\gamma_3 & -\gamma_2 & -1 \end{bmatrix} \begin{bmatrix} 1 \\ Z_{1t} \\ Z_{2t} \end{bmatrix} + \begin{bmatrix} U_{1t} \\ U_{2t} \end{bmatrix} = 0 \qquad (3.11)$$

It should be noted that both Wagner and Ladd have chosen similar normalization constraints in their systems. The experiments performed by Wagner were somewhat more extensive than those of Ladd. One hundred samples each with twenty observations were performed with two models distinguished by the variance–covariance matrix of the errors.[o] The predetermined variables consist of a trend variable and the endogenous variable, Y_2, lagged one period

The results show the bias of DLS to vary according to which structural coefficient is being estimated. Even though LISE estimates may differ greatly from the true value, confidence interval estimates using a t-distribution provide reliable inferences. In all cases the LISE estimates had smaller bias than their DLS counterparts, but greater variance. The IVE estimator (using the exogenous variable as instrument) is not consistent. When the correlation between U_{1t} and U_{2t} is small (Model 1), IVE is better than LISE, using bias and variance of the estimates as criteria; however, with increases in the absolute magnitude of the error's correlation, LISE is better than IVE. Finally, on the basis of root mean squared errors of the structural coefficients, both LISE and DLS appear equally good, since the low bias of LISE offsets its rather large variance and the reverse occurs with DLS.

In 1959, Neiswanger and Yancy [123] presented a most interesting study

_____

[o]The primary distinction between the two error structures is the size of the simple correlation between U_{1t} and U_{2t}. For Model 1 it is 0.50, while for Model 2 it is 0.99.

with Ladd's model to investigate the effect of "autonomous growth" on DLS and LISE. They note:

> The objective is to show how disparate rates of growth in economic time series may affect the estimates if those disparate rates of growth in endogenous variables are in part due to what we call *autonomous growth.* Autonomous growth is a secular change in the endogenous variables and parameters of the structural equations.[14]

Two experiments are performed each with one hundred and twenty samples with twenty-five observations. In the first set the predetermined variables and errors are independent, while in the second, time trends are added to each, imparting positive correlations between them.

Another feature which distinguishes this study from that of all other sampling experiments (except Mosbaek and Wold [113]) is that the set of predetermined variables does not remain constant across the samples of a given experiment. While they come from the same population, they do *not* attain the same values.[15]

Two models are applied to the both sets of data. The first is simply the Ladd model and the second includes a simple trend variable in each equation to attempt to account for the autonomous growth. Results are presented for both the estimated structural parameters and the estimated standard errors—the mean, standard deviation and root mean squared error of the first and means of the second.

Use of the first model without the autonomous growth effects shows DLS to have larger bias but smaller variance than LISE. Even with the root mean squared error LISE appears slightly superior to DLS. When the data with autonomous growth was used with the first model, LISE is not uniformly superior to DLS. The two techniques appear to be on a more equal basis. However, use of model two with the time trend once again gives LISE the advantage over DLS.

The authors find that the inclusion of a time trend variable, even without autonomous growth, will not worsen the estimates of either approach.

Until Nagar's [116] work, evaluations had been confined for the most part, to ordinary least squares on the structural form and limited information single equation estimators.[p] Four methods of estimation are considered in Nagar's experiments. They are: DLS, two stage least squares (2SLS), the unbiased second moment estimator (U2M), and the minimum second moment estimator.[q] His

---

[p]This statement should not be overly surprising, since other techniques were in the development stages during this period, and therefore remained unknown.

[q]All of these techniques are members of the k-class developed by Nagar [115] in 1959. The values for k which yield U2M and M2M are given as follows:

$$k = 1 + x/T \text{ (if } x = 0, \text{ estimator is DLS}$$
$$x = 1, \text{ estimator is 2SLS}$$

experiments are performed using Wagner's model (without intercepts). It is interesting to note that this model is in a real sense different from most previous models and many of those used in studies which have followed. The inclusion of a current and a lagged value for an endogenous variable as regressors in the second equation makes the estimated coefficients particularly sensitive to the values of k (the parameter of the k-class).[16] Nagar's experimental design conformed to that of Wagner. However, in contrast to Wagner, he estimated both equations in the model. DLS is shown to have greater bias than the other methods, but continues to have the smallest sampling variance. The mean squared error for DLS exceeds that of the other estimators in twelve of sixteen cases. 2SLS was shown to have the smallest bias, less than U2M, which is theoretically derived to have the smallest bias of the k-class (at a given level of approximation). This result may seem strange. However, both U2M and M2M require that the predetermined variables be composed solely of exogenous factors and it has already been noted that Z_2 in the Wagner model is Y_2 lagged one period.

Nagar summarizes the results in terms of the values of k and corresponding results. The bias in the estimates seems to decrease slightly with increases in the value of k, while the second moment of the estimates around the mean remains relatively stable.

The first explicit reference to the effect of structure on estimator performance was developed by Quandt [131] [132].[r] In addition to investigating the effects of multicollinearity upon members of the k-class, he outlines a series of experiments to test the hypothesis that the magnitude of the bias in estimates of structural coefficients is a decreasing function of the "sparseness" of the coefficient matrix associated with the endogenous variables.[s] Sixteen experiments each with one hundred samples of twenty observations are performed to

---

where for U2M $x = \wedge - (m + L) - 1$
       for M2M $x = \wedge - 2(m + L) - 3 - tr(C_2 Q)/tr(C_1 Q)$

T = *number of observations*
$\wedge$ = number of predetermined variables in the system
m = number of codetermined variables in the equation to be estimated
L = number of predetermined variables in the equation to be estimated
C_2 = partition of covariance matrix (C) of reduced form errors
C_1 = another partition of covariance matrix (C) of reduced form errors
      $(C = C_1 + C_2)$

$$Q = \begin{bmatrix} \bar{Y}^T \bar{Y} & \bar{Y}^T x_1 \\ x_1^T \bar{Y} & x_1^T x_1 \end{bmatrix}^1$$

x_1 = included predetermined variables
$\bar{Y}$ = systematic part of the codetermined variables

[r]Another interesting feature of Quandt's unpublished paper is his detailed treatment of the criteria for evaluation of the performance of the k-class techniques. Moreover, he introduces a variety of distributional measures which are not subject to the shortcoming Basmann attributes to mean squared error in cases where the degree of over-identification is not substantial (i.e., greater than three).

[s]Sparseness is measured by the frequency of zero elements in this coefficient matrix, as well as by their overall disposition in the matrix array.

evaluate the techniques. The experiments are distinguished by the degree of over-identification of the equation in the model which is estimated, the degree of multicollinearity, and the sparseness in the endogenous variables' coefficient matrix.

Equation (3.12) presents the basic four-equation model. The first equation is estimated and the estimates of its parameters form the basis of Quandt's evaluation of the k-class technique (e.g., from values of all k from -0.4 to 2.0 in units of 0.1).

$$\begin{bmatrix} 1 & -\beta_{12} & \beta_{13} & -\beta_{14} \\ -\beta_{21} & 1 & \beta_{23} & \beta_{24} \\ \beta_{31} & -\beta_{32} & 1 & \beta_{34} \\ \beta_{41} & \beta_{42} & -\beta_{43} & 1 \end{bmatrix} \begin{bmatrix} Y_{1t} \\ Y_{2t} \\ Y_{3t} \\ Y_{4t} \end{bmatrix} +$$

$$\begin{bmatrix} \gamma_{11} & \gamma_{12} & \gamma_{13} & 0 & 0 & 0 \\ 0 & -\gamma_{22} & 0 & 0 & -\gamma_{25} & 0 \\ 0 & 0 & \gamma_{33} & \gamma_{34} & \gamma_{35} & 0 \\ 0 & 0 & -\gamma_{43} & 0 & -\gamma_{45} & -\gamma_{46} \end{bmatrix} \begin{bmatrix} Z_{1t} \\ Z_{2t} \\ Z_{3t} \\ Z_{4t} \\ Z_{5t} \\ Z_{6t} \end{bmatrix} + \begin{bmatrix} U_{1t} \\ U_{2t} \\ U_{3t} \\ U_{4t} \end{bmatrix} = 0 \qquad (3.12)$$

The introduction of an additional exogenous variable into the second equation overidentifies the first equation. Four degrees of sparseness ranging from 100 percent nonzero elements to 44 percent and two degrees of multicollinearity constitute the other two distinguishing characteristics of his experiments.

Quandt finds that it is possible to reject the null hypothesis of no relation-ship between the mean absolute bias and sparseness. Moreover, the result appears more clearcut with DLS than with 2SLS. Comparisons of DLS and 2SLS results indicate that the latter technique appears to provide small sample distributions of any given coefficient which are more dense at the true value than DLS, but have "thicker" tails.

The effects of multicollinearity upon DLS and 2SLS from experimental results conform to the Klein–Nakamura [87] theoretical results. That is, " . . .

the presence of multicollinearity tends to affect two stage least squares relatively more unfavorably than direct least squares."[17] Overall, the choice between the two techniques under the conditions considered is not clear.

Prior to a paper by Robert Summers [166], the range of estimators considered in the Monte Carlo studies was limited to single-equation techniques. In 1965, Summers reported the results of a comprehensive set of experiments to evaluate: DLS, 2SLS, LISE, the full-information maximum-likelihood estimator (FIML), and least squares applied to the unrestricted reduced form (LSRF). The model within which these techniques were studied " . . . was deliberately made economically anonymous, with no direct real-life counterpart . . . so an appraisal of the estimating methods . . . would have general applicability."[18] The basic model can be written as follows:

$$\begin{bmatrix} 1 & \beta_{12} \\ 1 & \beta_{22} \end{bmatrix} \begin{bmatrix} Y_{1t} \\ Y_{2t} \end{bmatrix} + \begin{bmatrix} \gamma_{11} & \gamma_{21} & 0 & 0 \\ 0 & 0 & \gamma_{23} & \gamma_{24} \end{bmatrix} \begin{bmatrix} Z_{1t} \\ Z_{2t} \\ Z_{3t} \\ Z_{4t} \end{bmatrix} + \begin{bmatrix} U_{1t} \\ U_{2t} \end{bmatrix} = 0 \qquad (3.13)$$

The estimators were compared on the basis of three separate types of performance patterns: (a) conditional predictions of the dependent variables (b) structural coefficients estimates and (c) Studentized estimates of the structural coefficients. Twelve experiments were conducted in which variations in the: multicollinearity, sample size, and misspecification errors were considered

The results of all experiments show DLS to be inferior to the other techniques. The bias of DLS is so large that it overcomes DLS's relative advantage of low variance, and as a result the mean squared error of DLS estimates is much larger than that of the other methods. With regard to sample size, Summers' results indicate that under small sample conditions the consistent estimators' root mean squared error is approximately inversely proportional to the square root of the sample size. FIML is found to perform better than the other techniques, when its assumptions are fulfilled. However, the presence of misspecification has severe effects upon its performance. 2SLS is the most stable technique and LISE's performance seems to be quite erratic.[t]

One overall conclusion which can be derived from Summers' study is that while many sources of problems were investigated both alone and in their joint effects, the results of any one problem cannot be unquestionably isolated. Small changes in the character of the data or the specification of the structure can

---

[t]This observation seems to be consistent with Marino and Sawa's [147] findings from analytical results. See Chapter 2.

have appreciable effects upon the relative performance of the estimating techniques.

Schink and Chiu [148] have sought to identify the effects of model failures upon the estimators through the use of analysis of variance. They investigate the significance of varying degrees of autocorrelation and multicollinearity upon the performance of DLS, 2SLS, and LISE. Accordingly, the authors designed a series of experiments amenable to the ANOVA model, using a model similar to Wagner [174]. Multicollinearity is given a broader definition than in previous studies, where pair-wise correlations were used as indicators of it. Correlation between all exogenous variables of the model, both those within a given equation as well as variables of the other equations, is the measure. Thus, their approach is similar to one proposed by Farrar and Glauber [43]. Autocorrelation is generated by a first-order autoregressive scheme with varying degrees of association between the current disturbance and that of the previous period.

Schink and Chiu perform a two-way ANOVA with each of three criteria: bias, root mean squared error, and standard error of the estimated coefficients, to isolate both the separate and interaction effects exerted by autocorrelation and multicollinearity upon the estimators. Their results indicate that according to all three criteria DLS is greatly affected by both autocorrelation and multicollinearity. Using all three criteria, LISE was not significantly affected by autocorrelation. However, multicollinearity did significantly affect its performance pattern. When the root mean squared error and standard error were used for the ANOVA, 2SLS and LISE's responses to the two factors are similar. The pattern is quite different with bias; only half of the 2SLS estimates of the parameters exhibit significant effects from multicollinearity and autocorrelation when bias is a criterion.

The results of these studies reinforce our anticipations that DLS performance pattern under small sample conditions is likely to be worse than that of the consistent techniques. However, alterations in the degree to which the assumptions of the theoretical model are fulfilled can reverse this conclusion. The results are specific to the structures investigated and sensitive to them.

3.5 Simultaneous Equation Estimators:
Cragg's Work

In the late sixties, John Cragg reported the results of a comprehensive set of experiments he had performed to evaluate an extensive array of estimators including DLS, 2SLS, LISE, U2M, FIML, and three stage least squares (3SLS).[19] Since his experiments covered a broad array of problems, we shall focus upon each in terms of their order of appearance in publication.

The model used for all of his experiments is a three-equation structure given in Equation (3.14).

$$
\begin{bmatrix} 1 & \beta_{12} & \beta_{13} \\ \beta_{21} & 1 & 0 \\ 0 & \beta_{32} & 1 \end{bmatrix} \begin{bmatrix} Y_{1t} \\ Y_{2t} \\ Y_{3t} \end{bmatrix} +
$$

$$
\begin{bmatrix} \gamma_{11} & \gamma_{12} & 0 & 0 & \gamma_{15} & 0 & 0 \\ \gamma_{21} & 0 & \gamma_{23} & 0 & \gamma_{25} & 0 & \gamma_{27} \\ \gamma_{31} & 0 & \gamma_{33} & \gamma_{34} & 0 & \gamma_{36} & 0 \end{bmatrix} \begin{bmatrix} Z_{1t} \\ Z_{2t} \\ Z_{3t} \\ Z_{4t} \\ Z_{5t} \\ Z_{6t} \\ Z_{7t} \end{bmatrix} + \begin{bmatrix} U_{1t} \\ U_{2t} \\ U_{3t} \end{bmatrix} = 0 \tag{3.14}
$$

The first set of experiments, [24], investigate the sensitivity of the techniques to the stochastic assumptions of the model. The four types of violation were: (a) errors of measurement in the exogenous variables, (b), stochastic coefficients, (c) heteroskedastic disturbances, and (d) autocorrelated disturbances. Thirteen experiments each with fifty samples of twenty observations were conducted to evaluate these problems. The basic experiment was performed with an exogenous data set with low collinearity and resulted in the following conclusions. First, bias was not a serious problem for the techniques other than DLS. The perform-ance patterns of the estimators were not greatly different. In fact, using Kendall's coefficient of concordance to measure the agreement in estimator rankings, Cragg found the sums over the replications of the ranks of the estimates of each coefficient did not exhibit coefficients over 0.5. Since Kendall's coefficient may be interpreted (approximately) as a percent of perfect agreement, this finding indicates low overall consistency in performance. In general, the estimators can be grouped in three categories: (1) FIML and 3SLS (2) 2SLS, U2M and LISE and, (3) DLS. The weakness of DLS stems primarily from its bias. Finally, the standard errors of the consistent estimators were reasonably good for making inferences about the true values of the structural coefficients; those of DLS were not as useful.

Four degrees of measurement errors, differentiated by the variance in the errors, were added to all exogenous variables. While these errors increased the dispersion in the estimates of the structural coefficients of the techniques, such errors did not affect the reliability of the estimated coefficient's standard errors. Moreover, they did tend to bring the system estimators closer in performance patterns to the single-equation simultaneous techniques, and DLS's estimates improved slightly.

The introduction of stochastic coefficients had more dramatic effects. Stochastic elements were added to coefficients of regressors with each equation in the model. The errors had mean zero and different-sized variances for each of three experiments. The results indicate that stochastic coefficients affect the central tendencies of all the techniques. The relative standing of the estimators was altered, with FIML becoming one of the worst techniques and DLS one of the best.

Finally, two types of heteroskedasticity and three degrees of autocorrelation were investigated *separately*. Neither factor seemed to affect the central tendencies of the estimators or their relative positions. Autocorrelation did affect the Student-t ratio for DLS and 2SLS, U2M and LISE. In the first case, it caused a reduction in the number of unreliable ratios, and in the second, increases.

In his second paper, Cragg [25] reports the results of twenty-five experiments in addition to the basic one discussed previously. He considers (a) the collinearity in the exogenous variables (six degrees), (b) the values of the structural coefficients (eight sets), (c) the correlations between structural disturbances (two levels), (d) the size of the variance in the structural disturbances (five sets), and finally the number of observations (20, 35, 50, 70). The estimators were evaluated from their estimates of the structural coefficients. Rank totals of the estimates by each technique according to the absolute proximity of the estimate to the true value, in most of the experiments, suggested that FIML and 3SLS had the lowest rank totals; 2SLS, U2M, and LISE were next; and DLS had the largest totals. Inconsistencies between the ranks by separate coefficients within and between equations necessitates measuring the amount of difference or consistence in estimator performance across trials. The differences in performance patterns attributed to each technique were not pronounced. Cragg found that the results do depend on which structure, exogenous data set, and error structure were used.

In his third paper, Cragg [26] reports an evaluation of the estimators based upon their reduced form coefficients. That is, the structural estimators are evaluated based upon the *restricted* reduced form coefficients derived from their structural estimates and compared with LSRF (i.e., least squares on the reduced form). The same basic model is used and twenty-three experiments in addition to his basic experiment were performed. Sample size, coefficient structure, three degrees of multicollinearity, magnitude of error correlations, errors in the exogenous data, stochastic coefficients, heteroskedastic disturbances, and autocorrelated errors were all considered.

The estimators were judged on the basis of the absolute deviations of their estimates of the reduced form coefficients relative to the true values. DLS and

LSRF were found to be weaker than the other methods and 3SLS and FIML were stronger. Most of the variations in the basic model did not alter the overall ranking of the techniques. However, the presence of stochastic coefficients tended to improve the relative performance of LSRF and to deteriorate that of 3SLS.

Cragg's [27] final paper is an outgrowth of a controversy over our ability to estimate, in a meaningful way, the structural coefficients of economic models. This interesting methodological controversy was introduced into the literature in 1958 by T.C. Liu [99]. Liu argued that econometric models were merely approximations to reality. They "partialize" the true general equilibrium nature of the real world by limiting the number of variables included in each equation and in the system as a whole. Thus, the equations within a model are not the complete set. Three important consequences result. (1) Zero restrictions commonly used for identification are likely to be incorrect. (2) The number of equations in the model has been understated so that the constraint upon the number of prior restrictions and the number of equations is not in fact satisfied. (3) Finally, few variables are truly exogenous to the complete system.

Fisher [46] demonstrated that the use of *a priori* restrictions which hold only approximately, do not lead to the abandonment of simultaneous equation methods of estimation. While it is true that the use of them leads to inconsistent estimates, this property is an asymptotic one, and if the approximations are good enough, the consequences are likely to be negligible.

Five types of specification errors are investigated in Cragg's research. They include: (1) the omission of important variables from some of the equations, (2) specification of zero values for coefficients whose true values were near zero (i.e., the Liu-Fisher debate), (3) omission of an exogenous variable, (4) omission of an equation, and finally (5) failure to make use of all exclusion restrictions. For the most part the experiments were conducted with the same basic model, although for error type (4), the model was enlarged to a four-equation structure and the last equation was omitted. Each experiment contained fifty samples of twenty observations and the same basic estimators were studied (i.e., DLS 2SLS, U2M, LISE, 3SLS, and FIML). Both structural and reduced form coefficients were considered in his evaluations.

Several summary statements are possible in each case. The omission of important effects (e.g., specifying structural coefficients to be zero when they are of substantial magnitude) had pronounced effects on the estimates of the equations in which the misspecified coefficients occurred. While the medians of the estimates were affected the most, the dispersions were also changed. The relative standings of both FIML and 3SLS deteriorated for both the incorrectly specified equations and the correct ones. Thus, it would seem that single-equation techniques are to be preferred when there is some misspecification in the system. While the harmful effects of this type of misspecification carried over to the reduced form coefficients, they did not deteriorate sufficiently to make LSRF unquestionably the best estimator of these coefficients.

The second problem, that of specifying small nonzero coefficients to be zero in order to identify the simultaneous system, provided results in support of Fisher's [46] asymptotic findings. The estimates of those coefficients which were not specified to be zero were only marginally inferior to those derived when the zero restrictions were valid. Moreover, the use of "almost correct information" seemed to allow the structural estimators to provide estimates of the reduced form coefficients which were better than that derived from correct specifications via LSRF.

The omission of an exogenous variable had little effect upon the relative standings of the estimators. There was some deterioration in the full-model methods relative to the k-class techniques. In addition, the specifications which omitted equations had little effect upon the relative performance patterns of the estimators. While it affected the central tendencies of the techniques to some extent, the dispersions were not appreciably changed.

The last type of specification error considered by Cragg was the failure to use all *a priori* information. This problem did affect the performance of FIML relative to the k-class. Several "wild" estimates of structural coefficients in the underspecified equations were observed. However, these did not seem to result in very poor estimates of the reduced form. While all techniques were affected, the single equation simultaneous techniques remained appreciably better than DLS.

Serious specification errors did seem to have the greatest effects upon the system estimators (e.g., FIML and 3SLS). Nonetheless, LSRF was never unquestionably the best estimator of the reduced form, and the Liu [99] argument was not supported in these small sample studies.

3.6 Simultaneous Equation Estimators: Mosbaek and Wold's Experiments

Recently, Mosbaek and Wold [113] have reported the results of probably the most comprehensive set of experiments yet performed in the evaluation of the effects of: model size, sample size, multicollinearity, number of endogenous variables in a given equation of a simultaneous system, magnitude of the coefficients for the endogenous variables, error structure, and general correlation between predetermined variables in one equation and errors in another. The authors perform over fifty experiments each with one hundred samples. In contrast to previous work, for most of their experiments data for *both* the exogenous variables and the errors in all models were generated independently from sample to sample of a given experiment. Both sets of variables were derived from normal parent distributions. Consequently, their data generation procedure is similar to that of Neiswanger and Yancey [123], but quite different from the majority of past Monte Carlo studies where the data for the exogenous variables of a given experiment remained constant across the samples of that experiment.

Six basic sets of models were evaluated in their analysis. Since the results of their study are indeed voluminous, attention will focus here on a capsule outline of their experiments and a general overview of the results. The first set of models is a group of two-equation structures in which the magnitude of the coefficients of the endogenous variables distinguishes six of the experiments, and those remaining have equation sizes of two, five, and seven. The second group holds the coefficient magnitude constant and evaluates the number of equations. Consideration is also given to the number of exogenous variables in each given equation of a two-equation model. The third set evaluates sparseness in, and magnitude of the coefficients for the endogenous variables with a two-equation model. Group four evaluates the techniques using three popular, small-scale "realistic" models. The fifth set examines the effects of multicollinearity, lagged endogenous variables, sample size, and magnitude of the residuals. The sample size for most other experiments is forty observations. Variations between ten and eighty are considered. Finally, the last set examines the effect of correlation between predetermined variables of one equation and errors of another.

Four estimators are evaluated. They include: DLS, 2SLS, one iterative technique called fixed-point estimation (FP), and LSRF.[20]

The authors focus upon three basic sets of parameters: structural coefficients, reduced form coefficients, and coefficient of determination (R^2) for predictions outside the sample period (forty observations). The summary statistics on each of the structural and reduced form coefficients include the mean, standard deviation, and root mean squared error. Moreover, the mean of the asymptotic estimates of the estimated coefficients' standard errors is also reported.

With the basic two-equation model, ranking the techniques according to predictive power outside the sample period with R^2 as criterion reveals that 2SLS is best, DLS is worst, with LSRF and FP as intermediate cases. Alterations in the model reveal that: (1) the size of the coefficients for the endogenous variables is a very important factor in the relative predictive power of the estimators. When the coefficients are small, FP and 2SLS are not appreciably different in predictive ability; (2) the effects of sample size depend greatly on the model to be fitted. FP's performance appears to increase over the other techniques for most models, with increases in the sample size; (3) the predictive power of FP increases for a given model over other techniques with increases in the magnitude of the residuals; (4) DLS becomes a relatively better method when models become larger; (5) FP's performance deteriorates with increases in the number of variables in each equation, while 2SLS remains fairly stable. However, FP still remains better than either LSRF or DLS; (6) there was no appreciable effect upon the estimators with increases in the multicollinearity in the exogenous variables.

An evaluation of the techniques using the structural coefficients indicates that whatever the values selected for the coefficients of the endogenous variables, the small-sample distributions of 2SLS and FP are similar with approximate centering at the true value, while DLS has a slight bias. Unless the sample size is small, the bias in 2SLS is only slightly sensitive to the size of the endogenous variables' coefficients. DLS, on the other hand, is very much affected as is the FP estimator. The disperion of all three techniques increases with the size of these coefficients. One interesting finding with regard to LSRF is that the bias and dispersion in its estimates are relatively insensitive to the size of the structural coefficients for the endogenous variables.

Both FP and 2SLS appear to deteriorate relative to DLS as the size of the model increases. Decreases in sample size result in 2SLS being preferred over FP and DLS for structural estimation. Finally, increases in the residual variation improve the performance of FP relative to 2SLS. However, this preference is for a given coefficient matrix for the endogenous variables. Its effect upon estimator performance has been shown by Mosbaek and Wold to be substantial.

The preceding summary consists of a few capsulized remarks about a very large study. In general, the results reinforce the findings of Quandt on the effect of structure upon estimator performance. Cragg's results with regard to the lack of appreciable differences between estimator performance patterns are also reinforced. The relative merits of DLS versus 2SLS as shown in these studies are consistent with previous analyses, with one important exception. As model size increases DLS appears to have a fairly stable performance pattern, while that of 2SLS and FP deteriorates. Consequently, there may be reasons for preferring it. This finding generally contradicts most previous work in that the preference for at least single-equation simultaneous techniques was clear.[21]

3.7 Simultaneous Equation Estimators: Sasser's Approach

Another interesting approach to Monte Carlo evaluation of the econometric estimators has recently been introduced by Sasser [146]. His work is a logical extension of the work of Schink and Chiu in that he seeks to identify the effects of a number of factors upon the performance of three estimators—DLS, 2SLS, and LISE. Seven factors are enumerated as important determinants of the estimators' performance. They include: the number of observations, the number of equations, the extent of multicollinearity between the predetermined variables in the system, the percent of equations which are stochastic, the degree of simultaneity (measured in a graph theoretic mode), the degree of overidentification, and the number of exogenous variables. Of these seven, four factors were controlled in the experiments. These were: the number of equations, number of observatons, degree of multicollinearity, and percentage of stochastic equations. Three levels of each factor were examined, though a 3^4 factorial design was not possible.[u] Nine separate 3^2 factorial designs were constructed to study the number of observations and degree of collinearity. All other factors remained constant, except for the alterations in the percentage of stochastic equations and the number of equations.

Twenty replications of each experiment were performed and the normalized mean absolute deviation and normalized root mean squared deviation were used as the evaluation criteria for the techniques.[v] Explosive behavior similar to that reported by Summers [166] is found for LISE. This finding supports the theoretical work of Mariano and Sawa [104]. In general, the analysis of variance indicates that the number of observations is a statistically significant factor for both LISE and 2SLS, while multicollinearity is not. Neither factor appeared to affect DLS.

Regression analysis with truncated loss functions reveals some interesting findings. With LISE, the number of equations, number of observations, and degree of simultaneity were found to be significant determinants of statistical costs (normalized mean absolute deviation, normalized mean square deviation, and square root of normalized mean square deviation). For 2SLS, these factors, as well as the degree of multicollinearity and the extent of overidentification, were found to be statistically significant determinants of costs.

The regression results for DLS indicate that statistical costs are influenced by the percent of stochastic equations, degree of simultaneity, degree of over-identification, and the number of exogenous variables. Sasser's analysis is interesting because it represents the first attempt to measure the relative contribution of each of a number of determinants of estimator performance. While the results themselves do not provide insights beyond those available in previous studies, his methodology functions as a vehicle within which the diverse determinants of a simultaneous equation estimator's statistical cost function might be derived. As such, the research conforms to the approach advocated by Thornber [172] in his critique of previous Monte Carlo procedures.

In spite of fairly extensive experimentation, there remains a lack of definitive results in the evaluation of simultaneous equations estimators. Clearly, the multivariate nature of the loss functions associated with each forms the basis for the indecisive results presently available. Nonetheless, while conclusions of an all-

---

[u]His pilot experiment revealed that the uncontrolled factors dominated his four controlled variables.

[v]The normalized mean absolute deviation is the average of the absolute deviations normalized by the true parameter values, across parameters and replications. The normalized mean square deviation is the average of the normalized mean square errors across parameters and replicates.

encompassing nature cannot be ventured, several overall observations are possible. All techniques are sensitive to the simultaneity and size of the models within which they have been evaluated. If we can be assured that specification errors are not a problem and that there are substantial interactions in the system, then the system estimators are probably best, closely followed by the single-equation simultaneous methods.

3.8 Simultaneous Equation Estimators: Goldfeld and Quandt's Results

The final research set which will be briefly reviewed in this chapter is that reported by Goldfeld and Quandt [57] in a recent contribution to problems associated with nonlinear estimation in econometrics. The authors present sampling experiments for both single and simultaneous equation models in a most comprehensive analysis of nonlinear procedures. Two chapters are par-ticularly relevant to our present summary.[w] The first deals with the problem of autocorrelation in the context of a linear simultaneous-equation system; and the second considers the estimation of equation systems which are linear in param-eters but nonlinear in variables.

In the first case, Goldfeld and Quandt set up a two-equation model, as in (3.15), with a first-order process for each structural error.[x]

$$
\begin{bmatrix} 1 & \beta_{12} \\ \beta_{21} & 1 \end{bmatrix} \begin{bmatrix} Y_{1t} \\ Y_{2t} \end{bmatrix} + \begin{bmatrix} \gamma_{10} & \gamma_{11} & \gamma_{12} & \gamma_{13} & 0 \\ \gamma_{20} & 0 & 0 & \gamma_{23} & \gamma_{24} \end{bmatrix} \begin{bmatrix} 1 \\ Z_{1t} \\ Z_{2t} \\ Z_{3t} \\ Z_{4t} \end{bmatrix} + \begin{bmatrix} U_{1t} \\ U_{2t} \end{bmatrix} = 0 \tag{3.15}
$$

with:

$$
U_{1t} = \theta_1 U_{1t-1} + e_{1t}
$$

$$
U_{2t} = \theta_2 U_{2t-1} + e_{2t}
$$

---

[w]In Chapter 4, we shall also compare some of Goldfeld and Quandt's results with the estimation of linear probability functions to those resulting from the experiments discussed in the chapter.

[x]Y_{it} = endogenous variable, Z_{it} = predetermined variable.

Thirteen experiments each with fifty samples are performed to evaluate six estimators. The experiments are distinguished by the sample size, extent of the autocorrelation (i.e., magnitude of θ_1 and θ_2), simultaneity as measured by the size of β_{12} and β_{21}, the covariance structure of the structural errors, and the extent of collinearity present in the predetermined variables. The sample size ranges from 30 t0 180 observations. Moreover, interactions of these individual effects are considered.

The six estimators include DLS, 2SLS, and four different maximum-likelihood estimators. The first, designated FIML 1, maximizes the likelihood function associated with each equation individually in the presence of auto-correlation and is analogous to the Cochrane–Orcutt (CO) approach discussed earlier in this chapter. The second (FIML 2) ignores the autocorrelation and maximizes the likelihood function associated with the model. FIML 3 estimates the autocorrelation coefficients along with the structural parameters, and FIML 4 assumes we are given their true values and estimates the structural parameters.

The mean, mean squared error of the structural parameters, and mean of their estimated variances are considered in the evaluation. The shape of the likelihood surface and estimation of θ_1 and θ_2 are also discussed.

Their results indicate that the tradeoff between simultaneity and auto-correlation is, in fact, a real one. That is, if autocorrelation is severe and simultaneity "low," it is more important to take account of the former than the latter, and vice versa. In all cases, DLS produces the largest average bias in the estimation of the structural coefficients. Overall, the ranking of the techniques considered would be FIML4 and FIML3 as first, FIML1 second, FIML2 and 2SLS third, and DLS last. Low autocorrelation improves the ranking of DLS relative to FIML1. The ranking of the other techniques is somewhat sensitive to the problem at hand. That is, for low autocorrelation and strong simultaneity, FIML2 and 2SLS are more desirable than FIML1, since they account for the simultaneity.

Only two of these techniques estimate the autocorrelation coefficients, θ_1 and θ_2; FIML3 consistently understates their magnitude; with a few exceptions the same conclusion appears to characterize the other estimator FIML1.

In a second set of sampling experiments Goldfeld and Quandt examine the problems associated with estimation of nonlinear models. Three estimators are considered including DLS, a form of two-stage least squares, and a full-informa-tion maximum-likelihood technique.[22] The two-stage estimator is based upon Kelejian's [80] work and is constructed by regressing the right-hand side endogenous nonlinearities (i.e., the combinations of or transformations of endogenous variables) upon a polynomial in the predetermined nonlinearities. These polynomials should be of the same degree for endogenous nonlinearities of a given equation. The predictions from these equations are then used in the second stage of estimation aₔ instruments. Goldfeld and Quandt use polynomials of second degree for the two stage estimator (hereafter NTSLS).

Two models, given in (3.16) and (3.17) below, are used to evaluate the estimators.

$$\log Y_{1t} + \beta_{12} \log Y_{2t} + \gamma_{11} Z_t + \gamma_{10} + U_{1t} = 0$$

$$\beta_{21} Y_{1t} + Y_{2t} + \gamma_{21} Z_t + U_{2t} = 0 \qquad\qquad (3.16)$$

$$Y_{1t} + \beta_{12} Y_2{}^2{}_t + \gamma_{11} Z_t + \gamma_{10} + U_{1t} = 0$$

$$\beta_{21} Y_{1t} Z_t + Y_{2t} + \gamma_{20} + U_{2t} = 0 \qquad\qquad (3.17)$$

While the second model (i.e., 3.17) may be solved for a closed form in the endogenous variables, the first cannot. Consequently the data for the first is generated using an approximation procedure.[23]

This introduces error into the generated data with unknown characteristics, since the properties of the approximation scheme are not well-defined. However, the authors feel that, since the tolerance (10^{-3}) is fairly restrictive, these effects will be marginal.

A more important problem is that of multiple solutions. That is, there may be more than one set of values for the endogenous variables which satisfy the structural models. In fact, both models were assigned true values for their respective structural coefficients so that multiple solutions were produced. The effect of the choice of solution upon the estimators then becomes one of the factors examined in the sampling experiments. In addition to the selection of solutions for the first model, the sample size is varied (i.e., 20, 40, and 60 observations) to distinguish the experiments. For the second model, since only one set of solutions is in the positive quadrant, these are always selected.[y] The second model is also examined with two variance–covariance structures for the errors. Each experiment has one hundred samples and the evaluative criteria include the bias, mean absolute deviation, and root mean squared error of the structural parameters.

The results for the first model indicate that DLS is inferior in terms of bias, to the full information method and NTSLS. Moreover, the full information method is superior to NTSLS. Ranking the techniques by pair-wise comparisons also reinforces this conclusion. Only in the cases where the samples are a mixture of the two sets of solutions does DLS improve relative to NTSLS.

For the second model both the full information method and NTSLS are uniformly superior to DLS, and the ranking observed with model one of the full

---

[y]The first model has two sets of solutions in the positive quadrant, and the effects of selection of each individually, and a fifty-fifty mixture are discussed.

information method and NTSLS is preserved in this case. With increases in sample size these two become more comparable in performance.

An evaluation of the techniques based upon predictive performance with both models is generally in agreement with that based upon structural coefficients. Finally, with both models, DLS's performance deteriorates with increases in sample size while that of the other approaches improves.

Both of these studies are important contributions to our knowledge of the small sample properties of simultaneous equation estimators, since they address issues which have been ignored in all previous sampling experiments.

Table 3.4 summarizes the highlights of each study of simultaneous model estimators, including both its design features and definitive conclusions.

3.9 Summary

This chapter has reviewed a large, fairly diverse set of results for sampling experiments with both single and simultaneous linear equation systems. Since the studies have been outlined in tabular format at the end of each section, additional summaries of their specific results would be redundant. Rather, we shall highlight the areas within which small sample experimentation has taken place.

(1) A large number of studies have examined the estimation of single-equation models, with an error structure that follows a first-order Markov process. The results indicate that estimator performance is quite sensitive to the parametric specification. Moreover, in the absence of lagged endogenous variables in the estimating equation, the gains in efficiency resulting from accounting for this error structure *may not* be worth the estimation costs. The magnitude of the autocorrelation coefficient is an important parameter in that decision.

However, for those cases in which the model itself or a Koyck transformation includes the lagged dependent variable as a regressor, Dhrymes' iterative maximum-likelihood estimator seems to have the best performance pattern. Nonetheless, several other approaches, including Steiglitz and McBride's iterative estimator and three-pass least squares, have desirable performance patterns.

Experiments with second-order autocorrelation and Dhrymes' estimator indicate that it is more desirable to overspecify the order of autocorrelation, than to underspecify it.

(2) If we remove the assumption of normally-distributed error terms, then ordinary least squares does not remain the maximum likelihood estimator of linear single equation models. Moreover, if the errors follow a distribution without a finite second moment, then the Gauss–Markov theorem is not applicable. Experiments with a stable Paretian distribution favor the minimum absolute deviation estimator over OLS. Moreover, comparison of the two techniques when

Table 3.4
Tabular Survey of Monte Carlo Studies for the Estimation of Simultaneous Equation Systems[a]

Author	Size of Model	Size of Sample	Estimating Techniques Evaluated	Data Problems	Definitive Conclusions	No. of Trials
G. W. Ladd (94)	2 equations	30	DLS LISE	Measurement errors on variables	Little bias imparted to either estimator; greater bias, but smaller variance for DLS	30
Harvey Wagner (174)	2 equations	20	DLS LISE IVE	Two variance covariance structures, lagged endogenous variable	LISE had less bias and more variance; IVE better than LISE in Model I. DLS and LISE equally good by RMSE criteria	100
W. A. Neiswanger T. A. Yancey (123)	2 equations (same as Ladd)	25	DLS LISE	Effects of specification errors connected with the presence of time trends	On RMSE criteria LISE better than DLS. Inclusion of time when it is not needed has no appreciable effect upon either method, and may be desirable means of accounting for effects of autonomous growth	120
A. L. Nagar (116)	2 equations (same as Wagner)	20	DLS 2SLS U2M M2M	Two variance covariance structures	2SLS has smallest bias. Bias decreases slightly with increase in k for k-class estimators	100
R. Summers (166)	2 equations	20 40	DLS 2SLS LISE FIML	Variance covariance structures, structural specification, degree of multicollinearity	DLS inferior; 2SLS most stable; FIML good when assumptions fulfilled. LISE performs erratically	50
R. E. Quandt (131)	4 equations	20	DLS 2SLS k-class	Sparseness, multicollinearity	2SLS more sensitive to multicollinearity than DLS. Sparseness decreases bias; choice between DLS and 2SLS not clear	100

[a]This table is an expanded version of one presented in "A Comparative Tabular Survey of Monte Carlo and Exact Sampling Studies," *Australian Economic Papers*, Vol. 10, December 1971.

Table 3.4 (continued)

Author	Size of Model	Size of Sample	Estimating Techniques Evaluated	Data Problems	Definitive Conclusions	No. of Trials
J. G. Cragg (24)	3 equations	20	DLS 2SLS U2M LISE 3SLS FIML	Alternative variance covariance structures; errors in exogenous variables; stochastic coefficients heteroskedastic and auto-correlated errors	No method performed a great deal worse or better than others. Performance not greatly sensitive to violations of assumptions. Stochastic coefficients do affect the central tendencies of all estimators	50
W. A. Schink J.S.W. Chiu (148)	2 equations	25	DLS 2SLS LISE	Different degrees of multi-collinearity and auto-correlation	Analysis of variance of bias, RMSE, and standard error for the effects of problems on each estimator. DLS fares badly. LISE and 2SLS not affected by auto-correlation; significantly effected by multicollinearity	50
J.G. Cragg (25)	3 equations	20 35 50 70	DLS 2SLS U2M LISE 3SLS FIML	Multicollinearity structural changes, exogenous data, variance–covariance matrix of the errors (26 experiments in all)	Differences in estimators are not at all pronounced. DLS poorest, 3SLS and FIML better than 2SLS, U2M, and LISE	50
J.G. Cragg (26)	3 equations	20 35 50 70	LSRF DLS U2M 2SLS LISE 3SLS FIML	Multicollinearity, error covariance, errors in exogenous variables, stochastic coefficients, heteroskedastic errors, auto-correlation	Evaluation made in terms of the reduced form coefficients. DLS and LSRF found weaker than other methods, 3SLS and FIML strongest	50
J.G. Cragg (27)	3 equations	20	DLS 2SLS U2M LISE 3SLS FIML	Effects of misspecification errors	Effects of misspecification depended upon seriousness of mistake; omission of unimportant exogenous variable or equation affected estimators only slightly. Effect of serious misspecification was probably enough to render estimates useless. FIML most sensitive	50

E. Mosbaek and H. Wold (113)	2 to 7 equations	10 40 80	LSRF 2SLS FP DLS	Multicollinearity, size of coefficients for endogenous variables, error structure, endogenous and exogenous variables in given equation, lagged endogenous variables, model size and sample size	Focus on structural coefficients, reduced form coefficients, R^2 for predictions outside the sample period. Size of coefficients of endogenous variables important factor. DLS better with larger models. Sample size important. Magnitude of errors is also important. Small sample distributions of 2SLS and FP similar, DLS has slight bias	100
W.E. Sasser (146)	3, 6, 9 equations	20 40 60	DLS 2SLS LISE	Number of observations, number of equations, multicollinearity percent of equations stochastic, degree of simultaneity, degree of overidentification, number of exogenous variables	2SLS seems to be the best technique. 2SLS affected most by number of observations, number of equations, degree of simultaneity, multicollinearity and extent of overidentification. LISE affected by first three of these. DLS's costs determined by degree of simultaneity, percent stochastic equations, degree of overidentification, and the number of exogenous variables	20
Goldfeld and Quandt (57)	2	30 90 180	DLS 2SLS FIML1 FIML2 FIML3 FIML4	Examine the effect of first order autocorrelation in a linear simultaneous equation system; size of autocorrelation, strength of simultaneity, collinearity of predetermined variables and structural error's covariance	The techniques which account for both (FIML3 and FIML4) rank best, FIML1 is next autocorrelation is high, then FIML2 and 2SLS if simultaneity is not strong finally DLS	50
Goldfeld and Quandt (57)	2	20 40 60	DLS NTSLS Full information maximum likelihood with nonlinear model	Examine the estimation of simultaneous equation model which is nonlinear in variables; consider two models with alternative nonlinearities; choice of solution in generation process and error covariance structure examined	Full information method and NTSLS superior to DLS in both cases. DLS deteriorates with increases in sample size while the other improve	100

one (MAD) is maximum likelihood and the other (OLS) best linear unbiased indicates that the MAD criteria is more appropriate.

(3) The use of Zellner's seemingly-unrelated regressions estimator to estimate apparently-unrelated relationships has increased. Consequently, the small sample results derived for alternative specifications of this technique by Kmenta and Gilbert are quite important. In general, their sampling results indicate that the approach is always superior to OLS, so long as the errors are related and the regressors in each separate equation are not identical.

(4) Experiments with simultaneous equation models have progressed from two-equation structures to nine-equation structures. Moreover, explicit recognition of the problems resulting from multicollinearity, heteroskedasticity, autocorrelation, errors in variables, misspecification, simultaneity, magnitude of the errors, as well as several others have resulted in a variety of experiments. Their results indicate that insofar as we can rule out serious misspecification ranking the techniques as full information, single-equation simultaneous and nonsimultaneous is about the best that can be done. Choice within a category is difficult. If the system is large with few simultaneous links, the ranking may be altered.

(5) When autocorrelation is present in a simultaneous-equation system there is a tradeoff between the two in terms of which should be accounted for to assure "best" estimates. As one might suspect, with high autocorrelation and weak simultaneity, the former should be taken into account first. In the opposite case, account should be taken of simultaneity. In the absence of lagged endogenous variables, estimators which account for both are the most efficient, though the difference between them and the maximum-likelihood accounting for autocorrelation is not great.

(6) The estimation of a simultaneous-equation system which is nonlinear in variables presents a number of serious problems. The best general statement which can be made with limited evidence is that ordinary least squares on the structural form is a fairly poor estimator.

Notes

1. For a good description of these models see: Kmenta [90] pp. 473–95 and Rao and Miller [139] pp. 160–79.
2. See Thornber [172] pp. 801–806 for a convenient summary of these techniques. Also Copas [21] early Monte Carlo experiments revealed that corrections of the estimates from each of the techniques for bias increase the sampling variance.
3. See Dhrymes [31] pp. 99–139.
4. See Klein [82].
5. Rao and Griliches [138] p. 262. The symbols in the quote have been altered to conform to their corresponding parameters in the model.
6. While Sims [152] indicates that the examples chosen by Zeckhauser and

Thompson are probably subject to strong heteroskedasticity and this may have obscured the nonnormality question, it is nonetheless true that attention in both theory and practice is beginning to focus on errors with nonnormal error structures.

7. It should be noted that these results contrast sharply with the findings of Ashar and Wallace [6] with a model containing autocorrelated normal errors. Their experiment indicates the use of MAD meant " . . . one should be prepared to give up considerable efficiency . . . ". (p. 756).

8. See Kmenta [90] pp. 517–29.

9. See: Zellner and Huang [187], Zellner and Lee [188], Ferguson and Moroney 45], Kakwani [79], Parks [127], Telser [169], Powell [130], Smith and Fibiger [160], and Marcis and Smith [103].

10. For a complete statement of the assumptions of the model see Kmenta [90] pp. 517–529.

11. See Telser [169] and Kmenta and Gilbert [91], pp. 1183–1184. The Telser scheme is somewhat different than the others in that the disturbance estimates are explicitly entered into the equations of the system.

12. See: Kmenta and Gilbert [92] pp. 188–189.

13. Kmenta and Gilbert [92] p. 195.

14. Neiswanger and Yancey [123] p. 390.

15. Neiswanger and Yancey [123] pp. 392–393.

16. Nagar [116] p. 580.

17. Quandt [131] p. 31.

18. Summers [166] p. 4

19. Cragg's work was first reported in [23], and then subsequently published in a series of papers including [24], [25], [26], [27].

20. See: Wold [179], Dutta [36] and Maddala [100] for a further description of this estimator and other iterative approaches. The essential idea of the technique is to estimate every equation in the model with ordinary least squares, then the systematic part of each equation *individually* is used as the regressors for the corresponding right-hand side endogenous variables in a second round of ordinary least squares estimation. This procedure is continued until the estimated parameters from one iteration are not appreciably different from the previous round.

21. Quandt's [131] work is one exception to this. In addition Smith [154] [157] has found similar results. However, these will be discussed at greater length in Chapter 5.

22. See: Goldfeld and Quandt [57], pp. 233–234.

23. *IBID.*, p. 237.

4

A Single Equation Problem: Linear Probability Models Estimated With Binary Data*

The purpose of this chapter is to illustrate the Monte Carlo approach for evaluating estimators and test statistics within the context of a single-equation model. The assumptions of the model, problems under study, and design characteristics of our experiments are carefully reviewed so that the methodology discussed in previous chapters is outlined and the link between theory and experimentation becomes clear.

The first section of the chapter describes the usefulness of the linear probability model using illustrations from the current literature. It is followed by a discussion of the estimators for the model and the subset which are studied in this chapter. The third section discusses the design of our sampling experiments and data generation procedures. Sections four and five present and discuss the results, and the last section summarizes the chapter.

4.1 The Nature of Linear Probability Models

Many problems in economics and in other social sciences require the formulation of models with a dependent variable which is dichotomous. As survey research data accumulates, these models are likely to become increasingly important vehicles for explaining both individual and household decision making. Two recent examples may serve to illustrate their usefulness. The first of these is a study of the determinants of recreational behavior by type of activity. Cicchetti, Seneca, and Davidson [18] in 1969 used the 1960 and 1965 National Recreation Surveys in conjunction with data on the supply of recreation resources and facilities throughout the United States, to explain recreational behavior patterns in a two step approach. The first step estimates the determinants of the probability of engaging in a given activity and the second the expected number of days of recreation by each of the participants. Their results indicate that individuals' socioeconomic characteristics are important determinants of recreational behavior. Age, race, sex, and family income were found to be quite important. The estimated equations were then used to project future use in each of the activities studied.

---

*This chapter is based upon a set of sampling experiments conducted by Charles Cicchetti and myself. The complete results are available in: Smith and Cicchetti [159], and Smith [158].

Another recent study by Kain and Quigley [78] examines the determinants of home-ownership using a sample of 1,185 households in the St. Louis metropolitan area. A binary dependent variable (1 = own, 0 = rent) was regressed on a series of explanatory variables including measures of family size and composition, employment status, household income, and race. Their results were used as indicative of racial discrimination in home ownership, after accounting for both family characteristics and economic standing in the community.

The basic model underlying these studies suggests that the dependent variable, Y_i, takes on two values, one if the event occurs, and zero otherwise. Consequently, if we write the model as in Equation (4.1) with β a Kx1 parameter vector, X_i a 1xK vector of exogenous variables, and U_i the error, then we may interpret predictions from the model as conditional probabilities.

$$Y_i = X_i \beta + U_i \tag{4.1}$$

It should be clear that the nature of the model is such that the assumptions of the classical linear model of regression theory will not be fulfilled. However, Goldberger [54] has shown that if we are willing to assume that the expected value of U_i is zero, then we can derive the prerequisite error distribution and re-examine the model. For given values of X_i, Y_i may be either zero or unity. Accordingly, the corresponding values for U_i are either $-X_i\beta$ or $1 - X_i\beta$. If we wish the expected value of U_i to be zero, then we need only postulate a probability distribution for U_i which weights the respective values of U_i so that their sum is zero. Equation (4.2) designates this scheme.

$$P(U_i = -X_i\beta) = 1 - X_i\beta$$

$$P(U_i = 1 - X_i\beta) = X_i\beta \tag{4.2}$$

Therefore, the expected value of U_i is given in (4.3).

$$E(U_i) = (1 - X_i\beta)(-X_i\beta) + (X_i\beta)(1 - X_i\beta) = 0 \tag{4.3}$$

This specification, however, implies that the U_i are heteroskedastic. Their variance will be a function of the values of X_i as is seen in Equation (4.4)

$$
\begin{aligned}
\text{Var}(U_i) &= E(U_i^2) - (E(U_i))^2 \\
&= E(U_i^2) - 0 \\
&= (-X_i\beta)^2(1 - X_i\beta) + (1 - X_i\beta)^2(X_i\beta) \\
&= (X_i\beta)^2 - (X_i\beta)^3 + X_i\beta - 2(X_i\beta)^2 + (X_i\beta)^3
\end{aligned}
$$

$$= X_i\beta - (X_i\beta)^2$$

$$= X_i\beta (1 - X_i\beta) = E(Y_i) (1 - E(Y_i)) \tag{4.4}$$

Since $E(Y_i)$ is unknown, Goldberger [54] suggests a two-step procedure which uses the OLS (ordinary least squares) predictions of Y_i for $E(Y_i)$ and then applies an Aitken generalized approach. Moreover, McGillivray [107] has shown that this approach provides consistent estimates of β.

A second problem with the model under this assumed error structure concerns the distribution of the estimates of β. Since U_i is not normally distributed, the classical tests of significance are not relevant to the estimated coefficients. Nonetheless, all applications have made use of Student-t tests to assess the statistical significance of these coefficients. While McGillivray indicates that the Aitken estimates are best asymptotically normal, the relevance of this finding for most applications is not clear.

Finally, since predictions from the regression model are interpreted as probabilities, they should fall within the range of zero to one. The estimating technique, however, is not constrained so that such behavior is guaranteed. Consequently, arbitrary rules such as assigning values larger than one a value of exactly one and those less than zero, that of zero are usually adopted.[1] Regression analysis with this model is generally viewed as undesirable for the previously mentioned reasons. In a monograph on the analysis of binary data, Cox [22] notes that " . . . the use of a model, the nature of whose limitations can be foreseen, is not wise, except for very limited purposes."[2] However, the overall convenience of regression procedures, as well as the fairly high computational cost of alternatives, has induced most social scientists to continue using them in spite of their obvious limitations with this format.[3]

Given that regression procedures are to be used in the analysis of these models, then it becomes appropriate to ask whether or not the Aitken approach is worth the additional computational effort. Moreover, its very construction with the presence of OLS predictions of Y_i outside the zero to one interval has not been considered. The interpretation of test statistics including the Student-t test and coefficient of determination deserve attention. Thus, it would seem that there are a number of problems which might be examined in the context of this model.

4.2 Estimators for Linear Probability Models

The estimators for linear probability models with dichotomous dependent variables can be classified into three general categories. The first class includes the probit-like estimators. The essential idea underlying probit estimation is the construction of a new variable which represents the deterministic portion of the model in (4.1) The value of Y_i is then determined by comparison of this construct with a threshold variable, which is analogous to an error and is normally distributed with mean zero and unitary variance. Given this framework, it is possible to derive a maximum-likelihood estimator for the model and the predictions will be constrained to lie within the unit interval.[a] Another member of this general type of estimator is derived by assuming that the probabilities follow a logistic function, so that a logistic transform of the model provides a linear estimating equation.[b] When the data available for the model are binary dependent variables, estimation requires maximizing the derived likelihood function.[4]

A second approach to estimation of the model requires the use of a quadratic programming algorithim. The estimates in this case are derived by selecting them to minimize the sum of squared residuals subject to an inequality constraint upon the model's predictions. $X_i\hat{\beta}$ are required to fall within the unit interval. While this approach has some advantages, it also suffers from a primary shortcoming. The covariance matrix for the estimated coefficients is not clear.[5]

The last approach which was discussed briefly in the first section of this chapter consists of either OLS or GLS (generalized least squares) estimation of the equation given in (4.1). It is these techniques which will be evaluated in the sampling experiments reported in this chapter. As we noted, the construction of the GLS estimator requires the formation of an estimate of the error covariance structure from the OLS predictions of Y_i (i.e., $\hat{Y}_i$ = OLS prediction). If we allow the estimate of the variance of U_i to be given by Y_i $(1 - \hat{Y}_i)$, GLS will be a consistent estimator. However, there are likely to be the X_i's for which $\hat{Y}_i$ is outside the unit interval. In such cases, the estimates of the variance are inadmissible and there is no clearly defined procedure for the application of the Aitken approach.[6]

In what follows, three schemes for dealing with sample points which provide inadmissible variance estimates will be evaluated. Equation (4.5) describes the GLS estimators, where Σ is the OLS estimate of the error covariance structure, $\bar{X}$ is an $N \times K$ matrix of regressors (N = the number of observations), and Y is an $N \times 1$ vector of observations on the regressand.

$$b = (\bar{X}^T \Sigma^{-1} \bar{X})^{-1} \bar{X}^T \Sigma^{-1} \bar{Y} \qquad (4.5)$$

Σ^{-1} is a weighting function which can be illustrated graphically as a function of the corresponding values of $\hat{Y}_i$. Figure 4.1 plots Σ^{-1} for those predictions within the unit interval. The primary question which predictions outside the zero to one range raises is: what weight do we assign? Or in terms of the figure, the weighting function must be defined for $\hat{Y}_i$ less than zero and greater than one. Three weighting schemes will be examined. The first of these gives predictions outside the admissible range, which shall be designated hereafter as outliers, the smallest

---

[a]For a more detailed treatment, see Cragg [28] pp. 829–832.

[b]A logistic transform of a variable Z is given by log $[Z/(1 - Z)]$.

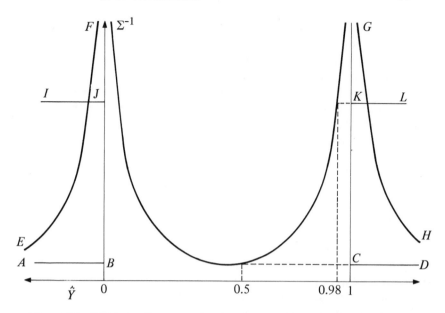

Figure 4.1. Weighting Functions Implied by Alternative GLS Estimators.

weight given to observations within the unit interval. This weight corresponds to that given to observations whose predictions equal 0.5. The Aitken estimator corresponding to this case will be labeled GLS1. The rationale underlying its weights implies that the informational content embodied in observations whose predictions fall outside the unit interval is small and therefore they should be neglected. In terms of Figure 4.1, we can display the weights corresponding to GLS1 by line segments AB and CD.

The opposite extreme to the GLS1 approach would be to assign large weights to outliers in order to improve the likelihood that Aitken estimated probabilities will fall within the unit interval. As representative of such cases,

Table 4.1
Weighting Functions for Aitken Estimators

Estimator	$\hat{Y}_i < 0$	$0 < \hat{Y}_i < 1$	$\hat{Y}_i > 1$
GLS1	$\dfrac{1}{(0.5)(0.5)}$	$\dfrac{1}{\hat{Y}_i(1 - \hat{Y}_i)}$	$\dfrac{1}{(0.5)(0.5)}$
GLS2	$\dfrac{1}{\lvert \hat{Y}_i(1 - \hat{Y}_i) \rvert}$	$\dfrac{1}{\hat{Y}_i(1 - \hat{Y}_i)}$	$\dfrac{1}{\lvert \hat{Y}_i(1 - \hat{Y}_i) \rvert}$
GLS3	$\dfrac{1}{(0.98)(0.02)}$	$\dfrac{1}{\hat{Y}_i(1 - \hat{Y}_i)}$	$\dfrac{1}{(0.98)(0.02)}$

GLS3 assigns weights to outliers corresponding to that given to $\hat{Y}_i = 0.98$. In terms of Figure 4.1, line segments IJ and KL present its weights for outliers.

A final scheme, intermediate to the previous two, would weight outliers according to the extent that the predicted $\hat{Y}_i$ is outside the unit interval. Thus, the further $\hat{Y}_i$ is outside the unit interval, the smaller weight will be assigned to the observation in question. One method which accomplishes this objective is to replace $\hat{Y}_i (1 - \hat{Y}_i)$ by its absolute value. The weights are given by EF and GH in Figure 4.1. This estimator is designated GLS2. Table 4.1 summarizes the three Aitken techniques' weighting functions.

4.3   Design of Experiments and Data Generation

In the first section of this chapter three problems were noted with linear probability models estimated from data with dichotomous dependent variables. The sampling experiments reported in this chapter were performed in order to shed some light on each of the questions implicit in these problems. They include: the relative efficiency of Aitken estimation versus OLS; the role of test statistics with the model; and finally, the impact of inadmissible predictions upon the model.

Twelve experiments each with fifty samples have been conducted to address these questions under a variety of conditions. Three general characteristics distinguish the experiments including: model, conditional error distribution, and sample size. Typically, studies with dichotomous dependent variables also include a number of binary regressors for such factors as race, sex, and any number of other qualitative variables to measure the attributes of the individuals, households, or firms sampled. Consequently, two different sets of regressors have been used for each of the error structures we investigate. The first, Model A, includes one continuous regressor and one binary regressor. The second, Model B, includes two binary independent variables. For each sample size, the values of the independent variables are constant across the samples of each experiment. Moreover, they remain fixed for the three error structures studied.

Table 4.2 presents the coefficient structures used to alter the conditional distribution of U_i which is a Bernoulli random variable. By altering the value of the intercept for each model, it is possible to change the distribution of U_i and therefore Y_i. The values of the intercepts differ across models A and B, in order that the expected proportion of zeros and ones in the sample might be held approximately equal, in spite of the difference in the regressors across the two models. Finally, the last distinguishing feature between the experiments is sample size. Each model and error structure was replicated with individual samples having twenty observations and one hundred observations. The total number of such samples within each experiment (i.e., the number of replicates) was held at fifty.

Table 4.2

Summary of Coefficient Structures

Model and Experiment	β_0	β_1	β_2	Approximate Proportion of Y's = 1[a]	Maximum Probability of $(Y = 1)$[b]
A					
1	0.25	0.25	-0.05	0.30	0.48
2	0.45	0.25	-0.05	0.50	0.68
3	0.65	0.25	-0.05	0.70	0.88
B					
1	0.16	0.25	-0.05	0.30	0.41
2	0.36	0.25	-0.05	0.50	0.61
3	0.56	0.25	-0.05	0.70	0.81

[a]This estimate is derived recognizing that the probability Y_i is equal one is equal to

$$\beta_0 + \sum_{j=1}^{2} \beta_j X_{ji}.$$

Substituting the mean values in the sample interval for each X_j we have the proportion reported above.

[b]These values are the maximum values for the probability Y_i will equal one across the sample interval for each experiment.

The specific form of the model used to generate the samples for each experiment is given in Equation (4.5).

$$Y_i = \beta_0 + \beta_1 X_{1i} + \beta_2 X_{2i} + U_i \tag{4.5}$$

For Model A, X_{1i} is a binary variable whose values were generated with a probability of a value of one of 0.50. In this case the values of X_{2i} were generated from a normal distribution with a mean of two and variance of unity. With Model B, the values of X_{1i} remain as previously indicated, while those for X_{2i} are replaced by values from a binary (0, 1) variable whose probability that X_{2i} equals one was 0.20. Since the values in both models were independently generated we do not expect problems of multicollinearity to interfere with the analysis.[c]

As Table 4.2 indicates, alteration in the value of the intercept, β_0, changes both the probability distribution for the error terms and their magnitude as well. The maximum probability that Y_i will equal one ranges between 0.48 and 0.88 in Model A and 0.41 and 0.81 in Model B. The errors were generated by first producing a sequence of pseudorandom numbers from a uniform distribution on the interval from zero to one and using these in conjunction with the inverse of the distribution function for U_i to generate specific values.[d]

[c]This statement should not be interpreted to mean that multicollinearity is not considered important, but rather that its effects are beyond the scope of the present research.

[d]See Appendix A for a more complete description of the methodology.

Table 4.3
Structural Coefficients: Results for Model A,
Sample Size—20 Observations

Exp.	Estimator	True Value	Mean	Bias	RMSE	Var
1	OLS	0.25	0.2290	−0.0210	0.2995	0.0893
	GLS1		0.2109	−0.0391	0.3111	0.0953
	GLS2		0.2195	−0.0305	0.2971	0.0873
	GLS3		0.2287	−0.0213	0.2730	0.0741
	OLS	0.25	0.2221	−0.0279	0.2145	0.0452
	GLS1		0.2411	−0.0089	0.2174	0.0473
	GLS2		0.2302	−0.0198	0.2128	0.0449
	GLS3		0.2201	−0.0299	0.2075	0.0422
	OLS	−0.05	−0.0439	0.0061	0.1000	0.0100
	GLS1		−0.0434	0.0066	0.1035	0.0107
	GLS2		−0.0423	0.0077	0.0971	0.0094
	GLS3		−0.0426	0.0074	0.0856	0.0073
2	OLS	0.45	0.4356	−0.0141	0.3201	0.1023
	GLS1		0.4326	−0.0179	0.3372	0.1134
	GLS2		0.4428	−0.0072	0.3189	0.1017
	GLS3		0.4456	−0.0044	0.3095	0.0958
	OLS	0.25	0.2217	−0.0283	0.2179	0.0467
	GLS1		0.2218	−0.0282	0.2199	0.0476
	GLS2		0.2164	−0.0336	0.2143	0.0448
	GLS3		0.2146	−0.0356	0.2132	0.0442
	OLS	−0.05	−0.0401	0.0099	0.1141	0.0129
	GLS1		−0.0373	0.0127	0.1238	0.0152
	GLS2		−0.0393	0.0107	0.1190	0.0140
	GLS3		−0.0393	0.0107	0.1155	0.0132
3	OLS	0.65	0.6501	0.0001	0.2932	0.0860
	GLS1		0.6576	0.0076	0.3033	0.0919
	GLS2		0.6453	−0.0047	0.2976	0.0886
	GLS3		0.6484	−0.0016	0.2856	0.0816
	OLS	0.25	0.2516	0.0016	0.2090	0.0437
	GLS1		0.2496	−0.0004	0.2167	0.0470
	GLS2		0.2509	−0.0091	0.2111	0.0445
	GLS3		0.2395	−0.0105	0.2145	0.0459
	OLS	−0.05	−0.0554	−0.0054	0.1122	0.0126
	GLS1		−0.0581	−0.0081	0.1164	0.0135
	GLS2		−0.0491	0.0009	0.1066	0.0114
	GLS3		−0.0520	−0.0020	0.0966	0.0093

Table 4.4
Structural Coefficients: Results for Model A,
Sample Size—100 Observations

Exp.	Estimator	True Value	Mean	Bias	RMSE	Var
1	OLS	0.25	0.2329	−0.0171	0.1155	0.0130
	GLS1		0.2463	−0.0037	0.1023	0.0105
	GLS2		0.2419	−0.0081	0.1007	0.0101
	GLS3		0.2391	−0.0109	0.1015	0.0102
	OLS	0.25	0.2373	−0.0127	0.1037	0.0106
	GLS1		0.2358	−0.0142	0.1011	0.0100
	GLS2		0.2349	−0.0151	0.1019	0.0102
	GLS3		0.2361	−0.0139	0.1014	0.0101
	OLS	−0.05	−0.0378	0.0122	0.0414	0.0016
	GLS1		−0.0437	0.0063	0.0358	0.0012
	GLS2		−0.0413	0.0087	0.0350	0.0011
	GLS3		−0.0405	0.0095	0.0345	0.0011
2	OLS	0.45	0.4587	0.0087	0.1258	0.0157
	GLS1		0.4611	0.0111	0.1240	0.0153
	GLS2		0.4569	0.0069	0.1275	0.0162
	GLS3		0.4568	0.0068	0.1277	0.0163
	OLS	0.25	0.2611	0.0111	0.1019	0.0103
	GLS1		0.2618	0.0118	0.1023	0.0103
	GLS2		0.2615	0.0115	0.1017	0.0102
	GLS3		0.2615	0.0115	0.1017	0.0102
	OLS	−0.05	−0.0522	−0.0022	0.0363	0.0013
	GLS1		−0.0538	−0.0038	0.0372	0.0014
	GLS2		−0.0514	−0.0014	0.0378	0.0014
	GLS3		−0.0513	−0.0013	0.0379	0.0014
3	OLS	0.65	0.6602	0.0102	0.1202	0.0143
	GLS1		0.6570	0.0070	0.1154	0.0133
	GLS2		0.6570	0.0070	0.1153	0.0133
	GLS3		0.6571	0.0071	0.1154	0.0133
	OLS	0.25	0.2451	−0.0049	0.0798	0.0063
	GLS1		0.2427	−0.0073	0.0802	0.0064
	GLS2		0.2427	−0.0073	0.0802	0.0064
	GLS3		0.2427	−0.0073	0.0802	0.0064
	OLS	−0.05	−0.0540	−0.0040	0.0437	0.0019
	GLS1		−0.0526	−0.0026	0.0423	0.0018
	GLS2		−0.0526	−0.0026	0.0423	0.0018
	GLS3		−0.0526	−0.0026	0.0424	0.0018

Table 4.5
Structural Coefficients: Results for Model B,
Sample Size–20 Observations

Exp.	Estimator	True Value	Mean	Bias	RMSE	Var
1	OLS	0.16	0.1321	–0.0279	0.1248	0.0148
	GLS1		0.1307	–0.0293	0.1293	0.0159
	GLS2		0.1348	–0.0252	0.1274	0.0156
	GLS3		0.1378	–0.0222	0.1278	0.0158
	OLS	0.25	0.2827	0.0327	0.1914	0.0356
	GLS1		0.2837	0.0337	0.1966	0.0375
	GLS2		0.2764	0.0264	0.1977	0.0384
	GLS3		0.2635	0.0135	0.1927	0.0369
	OLS	–0.05	–0.0135	0.0365	0.2936	0.0848
	GLS1		–0.0304	0.0196	0.3110	0.0963
	GLS2		–0.0229	0.0271	0.3020	0.0905
	GLS3		–0.0254	0.0754	0.2575	0.0606
2	OLS	0.36	0.3370	–0.0230	0.1351	0.0177
	GLS1		0.3368	–0.0232	0.1361	0.0180
	GLS2		0.3380	–0.0220	0.1371	0.0183
	GLS3		0.3417	–0.0183	0.1357	0.0181
	OLS	0.25	0.2793	0.0293	0.2404	0.0569
	GLS1		0.2793	0.0293	0.2414	0.0574
	GLS2		0.2765	0.0265	0.2425	0.0581
	GLS3		0.2674	0.0174	0.2362	0.0555
	OLS	–0.05	–0.0666	–0.0166	0.2939	0.0861
	GLS1		–0.0731	–0.0231	0.3176	0.1004
	GLS2		–0.0705	–0.0205	0.3090	0.0951
	GLS3		–0.0513	–0.0013	0.2471	0.0610
3	OLS	0.56	0.4976	0.0624	0.1379	0.0151
	GLS1		0.4973	–0.0627	0.1380	0.0151
	GLS2		0.4972	–0.0628	0.1383	0.0152
	GLS3		0.5048	–0.0552	0.1318	0.0143
	OLS	0.25	0.3328	0.0828	0.2078	0.0363
	GLS1		0.3359	0.0859	0.2140	0.0384
	GLS2		0.3325	0.0825	0.2096	0.0371
	GLS3		0.3201	0.0701	0.1999	0.0350
	OLS	–0.05	–0.0740	–0.0240	0.3464	0.1194
	GLS1		–0.0681	–0.0181	0.3700	0.1366
	GLS2		–0.0707	–0.0207	0.3684	0.1353
	GLS3		–0.0867	–0.0367	0.2838	0.0792

Table 4.6
Structural Coefficients: Results for Model B,
Sample Size—100 Observations

Exp.	Estimator	True Value	Mean	Bias	RMSE	Var
1	OLS	0.16	0.1612	0.0012	0.0550	0.0030
	GLS1		0.1621	0.0021	0.0550	0.0030
	GLS2		0.1627	0.0027	0.0550	0.0030
	GLS3		0.1629	0.0029	0.0551	0.0030
	OLS	0.25	0.2476	−0.0024	0.0652	0.0042
	GLS1		0.2459	−0.0041	0.0653	0.0043
	GLS2		0.2443	−0.0057	0.0646	0.0041
	GLS3		0.2437	−0.0063	0.0643	0.0041
	OLS	−0.05	−0.0422	0.0078	0.1148	0.0131
	GLS1		−0.0369	0.0088	0.1143	0.0130
	GLS2		−0.0369	0.0131	0.1092	0.0118
	GLS3		−0.0353	0.0147	0.1074	0.0113
2	OLS	0.36	0.3541	−0.0059	0.0923	0.0085
	GLS1		0.3539	−0.0061	0.0932	0.0086
	GLS2		0.3539	−0.0061	0.0932	0.0086
	GLS3		0.3539	−0.0061	0.0932	0.0086
	OLS	0.25	0.2492	−0.0008	0.1038	0.0108
	GLS1		0.2491	−0.0009	0.1039	0.0108
	GLS2		0.2491	−0.0009	0.1039	0.0108
	GLS3		0.2491	−0.0009	0.1039	0.0108
	OLS	−0.05	−0.0524	−0.0024	0.1273	0.0163
	GLS1		−0.0520	−0.0020	0.1266	0.0160
	GLS2		−0.0520	−0.0020	0.1266	0.0160
	GLS3		−0.0520	−0.0020	0.1266	0.0160
3	OLS	0.56	0.5596	−0.0004	0.0941	0.0089
	GLS1		0.5606	0.0006	0.0941	0.0089
	GLS2		0.5606	0.0006	0.0941	0.0089
	GLS3		0.5606	0.0006	0.0941	0.0089
	OLS	0.25	0.2430	−0.0070	0.0973	0.0094
	GLS1		0.2415	−0.0085	0.0980	0.0095
	GLS2		0.2415	−0.0085	0.0980	0.0095
	GLS3		0.2415	−0.0085	0.0980	0.0095
	OLS	−0.05	−0.0302	0.0198	0.1168	0.0133
	GLS1		−0.0358	0.0142	0.1102	0.0119
	GLS2		−0.0358	0.0142	0.1102	0.0119
	GLS3		−0.0358	0.0142	0.1102	0.0119

Table 4.7
Summary of Estimator Performance[a]

Estimator	N = 20 Bias	Var	RMSE	N = 100 Bias	Var	RMSE
OLS	3	5	5	8	$4\frac{9}{12}$	$5\frac{7}{12}$
GLS1	5			$4\frac{1}{6}$	$4\frac{1}{12}$	$4\frac{9}{12}$
GLS2	$1\frac{1}{2}$			$2\frac{1}{6}$	$4\frac{7}{12}$	$4\frac{3}{12}$
GLS3	$8\frac{1}{2}$	13	13	$3\frac{4}{6}$	$4\frac{7}{12}$	$3\frac{5}{12}$
Total	18	18	18	18	18	18

[a]This table presents the number of coefficients which are estimated best with each method according to each of the three criteria. If a tie occurred, each estimator was given the appropriate fraction.

4.4   Results of the Experiments:
Coefficient Estimates

Two types of measures of the performance patterns of OLS, GLS1, GLS2, and GLS3 estimators will be reported for each experiment. They are parametric and nonparametric statistics. Tables 4.3 through 4.6 present several summary statistics for each coefficient and estimator across all twelve experiments. In each case the sample mean, bias, root mean squared error (RMSE), and variance ($1/n$ $\Sigma \, (\hat{\beta}_i - \hat{\beta})^2$ are presented.[e]

In Model A with samples of size 20 using either RMSE or variance as criteria, GLS3 appears to be better than OLS and the other GLS techniques. With Model B this ranking still holds true, but the performance pattern of OLS seems improved relative to GLS3. Table 4.7 summarizes the results across both models for the three experiments, using each of three possible criteria to rank the techniques (bias, variance, and RMSE). The table reports the number of coefficients in which one estimator outperformed the others.[f]

Increasing the sample size to one-hundred observations has three effects. First, each technique's performance under all criteria improves, as we might expect, with increased sample size. Moreover, the parametric statistics (i.e., bias, RMSE and variance) for each estimator are, with but a few exceptions, one-half their former levels. Second, the perceived discrepancy between the performance of the three GLS techniques is virtually eliminated. Thus, the procedure to accommodate inadmissible variance estimates does not appear important with larger samples. Finally, the observed discrepancy between the GLS techniques and OLS

---

[e]See Appendix B for a description of each of these statistics and their meaning. In addition, it should be noted that some apparent inconsistencies in the table are the result of rounding to significant digits for tabular display.

[f]The total possible coefficient is eighteen. That is three in each model, two models and three error structures (i.e., $3 \times 2 \times 3 = 18$).

Table 4.8
Decentralization in Structural Coefficients (Percentage)

Model and Experiment	Sample Size	OLS β_0	OLS β_1	OLS β_2	GLS β_0	GLS β_1	GLS β_2
A							
1	20	22	10	34	24	12	34
	100	2	2	12	0	2	10
2	20	12	14	34	8	16	36
	100	0	0	4	0	0	6
3	20	2	12	30	2	12	32
	100	0	0	18	0	0	16
B							
1	20	8	4	48	8	4	48
	100	0	0	34	0	0	38
2	20	0	12	46	0	12	46
	100	0	0	28	0	0	28
3	20	0	8	32	0	8	32
	100	0	0	42	0	0	36

with samples of twenty observations is practically eliminated when the sample size is increased to one hundred observations.

Another aspect of the results that should be considered is Quandt's measure of extreme errors, decentralization, (the percent of times each technique's estimates had the wrong sign for the coefficients). Since there was no difference in decentralization across the GLS techniques, their performance is reported under one general heading of GLS. Table 4.8 reports these results. In nearly all cases, increased sample size greatly reduces or eliminates the decentralization that is present in samples of twenty observations. Furthermore, the pattern does not appear to differ appreciably across the estimators.

Another interesting aspect of the techniques' performance is the consistency in their rankings across the fifty trials of each experiment. Table 4.9 presents Kendall's coefficient of concordance for each structural coefficient in each experiment. This nonparametric statistic measures the agreement in estimator ranking (according to the absolute proximity of the estimate to the true value) for each OLS and each GLS technique across the fifty trials of each experiment. It is calculated by comparing the techniques' rank sum with what it would have been under perfect agreement.[g] The coefficient may be interpreted as the percent of perfect agreement in these rankings. Overall, as the table indicates, the rankings are not highly consistent for any of the GLS techniques. Moreover, it appears that the consistency declines with the larger sample size. While there are

---

[g]See Appendix B for more details.

Table 4.9
Consistency in Ranking of Techniques: Kendall's Coefficient of Concordance

Exp.	Estimator	Sample Size	Model A			Model B		
			β_0	β_1	β_2	β_0	β_1	β_2
1	GLS1	20	0.2304	0.0256	0.0784	0.2704	0.0016	0.1024
		100	0.0016	0.0064	0.0144	0.0576	0.0256	0.0256
	GLS2	20	0.0144	0.0256	0.0064	0.0576	0.0144	0.0400
		100	0.0000	0.0000	0.0256	0.0576	0.0016	0.0400
	GLS3	20	0.0000	0.0000	0.0016	0.0064	0.0064	0.7056
		100	0.0016	0.0000	0.0144	0.0400	0.0000	0.0400
2	GLS1	20	0.0256	0.0144	0.0784	0.0144	0.0144	0.1024
		100	0.0144	0.0144	0.0784	0.0000	0.0016	0.0400
	GLS2	20	0.0256	0.0400	0.0400	0.0064	0.0064	0.0256
		100	0.0144	0.0064	0.0576	0.0000	0.0016	0.0400
	GLS3	20	0.0016	0.0576	0.0064	0.0064	0.0000	0.2704
		100	0.0144	0.0064	0.0576	0.0000	0.0016	0.0400
3	GLS1	20	0.0000	0.0016	0.0144	0.0000	0.0144	0.1296
		100	0.0064	0.0144	0.0064	0.0000	0.0016	0.1024
	GLS2	20	0.0400	0.0000	0.0400	0.0256	0.0064	0.0064
		100	0.0144	0.0144	0.0064	0.0000	0.0016	0.1024
	GLS3	20	0.0576	0.0016	0.1024	0.0016	0.1936	0.5184
		100	0.0064	0.0144	0.0064	0.0000	0.0016	0.1024

some exceptions, this conclusion reinforces the results found previously. That is, the techniques do not exhibit appreciable differences in performance patterns with larger samples.

An additional aspect of the performance of each estimating technique is its estimate of the estimated coefficients' covariance matrix. The calculation of these covariance matrices is described in Equations (4.6) and (4.7).

$$\Sigma_{OLS} = \sigma^2 (\bar{X}^T \bar{X})^{-1} \tag{4.6}$$

$$\Sigma_{GLS_i} = (\bar{X}^T \Sigma_i^{-1} \bar{X})^{-1} \tag{4.7}$$

where:

$$\sigma^2 = \frac{1}{n-3} \sum_{i=1}^{n} (Y_i - \hat{Y}_i)^2$$

$\hat{Y}_i$ = prediction from OLS estimates

Σ_i = estimated error structure (i = 1, 2, 3 for GLS1, GLS2, GLS3 respectively).

The OLS estimates of the variance–covariance matrix for the estimated coefficients are known to be biased in the presence of heteroskedastic disturbances. GLS techniques, in principle, should provide asymptotically unbiased estimates of the estimated coefficients' covariance structure. Since the results hold true across all the coefficients in the two models, Table 4.10 presents only those for β_1 in models A and B. The mean of the fifty estimates of the estimated co-efficient's variance is compared to the corresponding mean squared error (the square of RMSE in Tables 4.3 through 4.6). The difference between the two provides some indication of the extent of bias in the respective estimators.

Overall, two observations are possible: (1) OLS and all GLS techniques provide biased estimates of the estimated coefficients' variance, and the magnitude of the bias appears to diminish with sample size; (2) the distinction between the three GLS estimators of the variance virtually disappears when the sample is increased to a size of one hundred observations. Moreover, the distinction between the OLS and GLS estimates is, at best, marginal.[h]

[h]Before proceeding to discuss other aspects of the results of these experiments, it would be desirable to compare the performance patterns of OLS and our GLS techniques found in our analysis with work reported by Goldfeld and Quandt [67] pp. 124–134. In their sampling study, four techniques including OLS, a generalized estimator based upon estimates of Σ from a restricted least squares approach (i.e., minimizing the sum of squares subject to the inequality restriction discussed earlier), a maximum-likelihood estimator based upon the error structure we discuss, and probit are evaluated.

Table 4.10
Variance Estimates for the Estimated Coefficient β_1

Exp.	Estimator	Sample Size	A		B	
			Mean	MSE	Mean	MSE
1	OLS	20	0.0383	0.0460	0.0346	0.0366
		100	0.0075	0.0180	0.0078	0.0042
	GLS1	20	0.0313	0.0472	0.0355	0.0387
		100	0.0069	0.0102	0.0070	0.0042
	GLS2	20	0.0272	0.0453	0.0320	0.0391
		100	0.0069	0.0104	0.0070	0.0042
	GLS3	20	0.0264	0.0431	0.0303	0.0371
		100	0.0069	0.0103	0.0070	0.0041
2	OLS	20	0.0518	0.0475	0.0468	0.0578
		100	0.0094	0.0104	0.0095	0.0108
	GLS1	20	0.0425	0.0484	0.0413	0.0583
		100	0.0092	0.0105	0.0090	0.0108
	GLS2	20	0.0419	0.0459	0.0393	0.0588
		100	0.0092	0.0103	0.0090	0.0108
	GLS3	20	0.0418	0.0455	0.0373	0.0558
		100	0.0092	0.0103	0.0090	0.0108
3	OLS	20	0.0404	0.0437	0.0422	0.0432
		100	0.0082	0.0064	0.0081	0.0095
	GLS1	20	0.0377	0.0470	0.0381	0.0458
		100	0.0083	0.0064	0.0081	0.0096
	GLS2	20	0.0361	0.0446	0.0338	0.0439
		100	0.0083	0.0064	0.0081	0.0096
	GLS3	20	0.0358	0.0460	0.0321	0.0399
		100	0.0083	0.0064	0.0081	0.0086

4.5 Results of the Experiments:
Test Statistics

As it was noted in Chapter 1, Monte Carlo studies need not be concerned solely with estimators and their performance patterns. There is also a need to evaluate the properties of test statistics. One recent example of a comprehensive sampling evaluation of tests for specification errors is a study by Ramsey and Gilbert] 135] . In our present case, there is also some scope for evaluating popular

---

With the Bernoulli error structure, OLS and the Goldfeld–Quandt GLS are roughly comparable with the appropriate maximum likelihood technique best and probit inferior. In the probit error model, probit is not unambiguously best and OLS, GLS, and the maximum-likelihood technique are all comparable. Consequently, these findings are generally consistent with our preference for OLS over Aitken techniques. Moreover, probit may not need to be considered for such models.

test statistics with linear probability models. Since the error structure is not normal, we do not expect, under small sample conditions, that the distribution of parameter estimates will be normal. Thus, application of Student-t tests for hypotheses related to the individual coefficients would not seem appropriate and strictly speaking, we ought to focus our attention upon deriving test statistics which are relevant to the model at hand. However, most applications of the model proceed with t-tests of the hypothesis of no association (i.e., $H_0: \beta = 0$), ignoring the assumed error structure. Kain and Quigley [78], for example, make some fairly strong statements concerning discrimination in the housing market, on the basis of these t-ratios. They note:

> . . . even after controlling for the differences in prior tenure, Negro house-
> holds are .09 less likely to become homeowners than white households in
> today's 'open housing' market.[7]

They are not the only ones; all studies using regression analysis for this model have relied upon the t-test. Our concern, here, is with the power of the test with OLS and GLS techniques under a variety of conditions.

Table 4.11 reports the percent of samples in which the null hypothesis that $\beta_1 = 0$ was rejected at the five-percent level. The results indicate that the power of the test is quite limited for small samples. Furthermore, there does not appear to be any difference in the performance of the test with each of the four techniques. With increased sample size the t-test becomes much more powerful. How-

Table 4.11
Student's t Test Performance ($H_0: \beta_1 = 0$): Percent of
Samples Rejecting the Null Hypothesis

Model and Experiment	Sample Size	Estimators			
		OLS	*GLS1*	*GLS2*	*GLS3*
A					
1	20	22	32	30	30
	100	72	78	76	78
2	20	18	22	22	20
	100	74	76	76	76
3	20	26	22	20	20
	100	70	70	70	70
B					
1	20	28	24	26	26
	100	80	84	84	84
2	20	26	26	26	26
	100	66	64	64	64
3	20	44	44	44	44
	100	66	64	64	64

ever, there are a number of other properties such as interval estimation with Student-t distribution, which might have been studied. These results are presented for illustrative purposes and should not be misconstrued as the only important aspect of use of the Student-t distribution.

An equally important problem with linear probability models, estimated with dichotomous dependent variables, is measurement of the goodness of fit of the estimated relationship. Neter and Maynes [125] have noted that:

> Even when the regression curve is linear, the significance of ρ^2 in the case of 0, 1 dependent variable is not clear. For the usual continuous dependent variable, one can guage a given value of ρ^2 against a maximum of 1. Not so when the dependent variable is of the 0, 1 type.[8]

Moreover, Morrison [111] provides, in a recent paper, a theoretical means of bounding the coefficient of determination for certain probability distributions for the predictions from a linear probability model. Accordingly, we shall examine the distribution of R^2 with our OLS estimates of the models discussed previously, comparing them to the "true" calculated value for each experiment. Equation (4.8) presents the formula for calculating the value of R^2, using the OLS estimates of each model, and (4.9) the expression for the true calculated value of the coefficient of determination (designated hereafter as RT^2).

$$R^2 = 1 - \frac{\sum_{i=1}^{n} (Y_i - \hat{Y}_i)^2}{\sum_{i=1}^{n} (Y_i - \bar{Y})^2} \tag{4.8}$$

where:

$\hat{Y}_i$ = predictions from OLS estimates

$\bar{Y}$ = sample mean of Y_i

n = sample size

$$RT^2 = 1 - \frac{\sum_{i=1}^{n} (U_i - \bar{U})^2}{\sum_{i=1}^{n} (Y_i - \bar{Y})^2} \tag{4.9}$$

where:

U_i = generated pseudorandom variates

$\bar{U}$ = sample mean of generated U_i's (not necessarily zero)

Table 4.12 presents the mean values of R^2 and RT^2 for each experiment. In addition, the mean sum of absolute deviations of the OLS estimates about their "true" values (MSAD) and Kendall's coefficient of concordance (w) are also reported.

The estimated R^2 appears to overestimate its true value for both sample sizes. However, the extent of positive bias seems to diminish with sample size. Moreover, the dispersion of the estimates about their corresponding true values (measured by MSAD) declines with large samples.

Since we cannot interpret a coefficient of determination of 0.05 as indicating that five percent of the total variation has been accounted for by the model, we might ask what use is the statistic? In order to assess its value as an index of relative association, i.e., as a means of discerning the goodness of fit of one equation relative to another, the estimated R^2 statistics have been ranked from highest to lowest in each experiment and compared to a similar ranking of the RT^2 statistics. The coefficient of concordance, (w), measures the strength of association in these rankings. This coefficient, as we noted earlier, may be interpreted as a percent of perfect agreement. Our results indicate very high agreement in the rankings.

Since RT^2 provides an indication of the systematic variation relative to the total variation in the model, this consistency in the ranking of R^2 with RT^2 would seem to suggest that R^2 may provide a good comparative index of fit. That is, if we are comparing one linear probability equation with another, R^2 may help us discriminate between them. This conclusion does *not* refute the work of Neter and Maynes [125] and Morrison [111]. Rather it reinforces their findings in that the estimated R^2 are bounded from above.

Table 4.13 presents the frequency distribution for R^2 for all our experiments. Several findings are of interest. First, the frequency distributions are concentrated around those values close to zero. With a sample size of twenty observations, for four of the six experiments the modal class is the first one (0.00 – 0.06). Moreover, the distribution becomes more concentrated around the first three classes with increases in the sample size. Finally, the median class falls within the first five classes for samples with twenty observations, and within the first two, when the sample size is increased to one hundred observations.

4.6 Conclusions and Summary

This chapter has sought to illustrate the considerations in designing, implementing, and analyzing a series of Monte Carlo experiments with a single-

Table 4.12
Coefficient of Determination: Some Parametric and Nonparametric Results

Model and Experiment	N = 20				N = 100			
	w	R^2	RT^2	$MSAD$	w	R^2	RT^2	$MSAD$
A								
1	0.898	0.1787	0.0612	0.1175	0.984	0.0993	0.0781	0.0212
2	0.910	0.1565	0.0588	0.0975	0.985	0.0990	0.0841	0.0149
3	0.901	0.2041	0.0925	0.1115	0.981	0.1011	0.0864	0.0147
B								
1	0.967	0.1894	0.1014	0.0880	0.970	0.0882	0.0745	0.0137
2	0.930	0.1717	0.0776	0.0941	0.986	0.0825	0.0626	0.0199
3	0.947	0.2080	0.1140	0.0940	0.987	0.0870	0.0673	0.0197

Table 4.13
Frequency Distribution for R^2

Class Interval	A						B					
	1		2		3		1		2		3	
	20	100	20	100	20	100	20	100	20	100	20	100
0.00 – 0.06	8	14	12	12	9	11	12	14	12	22	5	19
0.06 – 0.10	4	15	10	20	6	15	5	16	9	12	5	12
0.10 – 0.14	9	11	6	9	5	15	3	16	6	9	10	12
0.14 – 0.18	8	5	3	6	4	5	8	3	5	2	6	3
0.18 – 0.22	3	3	5	1	6	3	6	1	2	4	7	3
0.22 – 0.26	6	2	4	2	5	1	4	–	4	1	2	1
0.26 – 0.30	2	–	2	–	3	–	2	–	2	–	2	–
0.30 – 0.34	3	–	1	–	2	–	2	–	1	–	3	–
0.34 – 0.38	4	–	4	–	3	–	3	–	4	–	4	–
0.38 – 0.42	2	–	3	–	3	–	–	–	2	–	1	–
0.42 – 0.46	–	–	–	–	–	–	3	–	1	–	3	–
0.46 – 0.50	–	–	–	–	3	–	–	–	2	–	1	–
0.50 – 0.54	–	–	–	–	–	–	1	–	–	–	1	–
0.54 – 0.58	–	–	–	–	–	–	–	–	–	–	–	–
0.58 – 0.62	–	–	–	–	1	–	–	–	–	–	–	–
0.62 – 0.66	–	–	–	–	–	–	1	–	–	–	–	–

equation model. The problem of linear probability models estimated with dichotomous dependent variables was chosen because it represents a fairly timely topic in applied econometric research.[i] Moreover, it is a member of the class of problems dealing with the general linear model in the presence of nonnormal error structures.[j]

For the purpose of review, several points may be worthy of mention again.

(1) If we are prepared to accept the Bernoulli error structure derived under the assumption that $E(U_i) = 0$, there are three problems with regression analysis of the model.

    i.   The error structure is heteroskedastic.
    i.i. The nonnormal districution for the error makes classical tests of hypotheses with small samples of questionable value.
    i.i.i.Predictions outside the unit interval impose problems for a two-stage Aitken estimator for the model, since they yield inadmissible variance estimates.

(2) Three Aitken estimators are developed for handling outliers (i.e., predictions outside the zero to one range). They include:

    i.   Giving outliers small weight.
    i.i. Giving outliers weights according to the extent to which they are outside the unit interval.
    i.i.i.Giving outliers large weight.

(3) Twelve experiments, each with fifty samples, have been conducted to evaluate OLS and the three Aitken estimators. The experiments are distinguished by the character of the model, the conditional error structure, and the sample size.

(4) With a sample size of twenty observations, the GLS technique which gives large weight to outliers seems marginally better than the other approaches. This ranking is somewhat weakened for a model whose regressors are both binary variables. When the sample size is increased to one hundred observations, there are little apparent gains from Aitken estimation.

(5) The power of the Student's t-test for testing the hypothesis of no association with each estimated coefficient is very limited with small samples, irrespective of the estimator. An increase in the sample size results in a more

---

[i]Theil [170], pp. 628–636, considers research in this area as part of the "frontiers of econometrics." While we do not want to accord definitive stature to the preceding sampling experiments, they do provide some information on estimators for a growingly important class of problems.

[j]For a review of two other studies with nonnormal error structures, see Section 2 of Chapter 3.

acceptable performance for the test. R^2 tends to overestimate its true value with OLS estimates in small samples. The distribution of values for this index of goodness of fit in traditional models is clustered around values near zero. Preliminary tests indicate that R^2 may be a useful index of relative fit of two linear probability equations.

NOTES

1. See Huang, pp. 169–171, Kmenta [67,90] pp. 425–428.
2. Cox [22] p. 18.
3. See: Cicchetti, Seneca and Davidson [18] pp. 82–86 for more discussion, and Feldstein [44]. Moreover, a recent study by Cragg [28] pp. 835–836 of probit estimators reveals some problems in their application.
4. Linear probability models may also be estimated from aggregate time series data. However, such problems, in which the dependent variables are not dichotomous will not be of immediate concern to us. Lee, Judge, and Zellner [97] have reported on their application and some sampling results with them in a recent monograph to which the reader is referred.
5. See: Judge and Takayama [74] and Lee, Judge, and Zellner [97].
6. Huang [67] p. 170 notes that the selection of the appropriate weights for cases in which $\hat{Y}_i$ is outside the unit interval is essentially arbitrary.
7. Kain and Quigley [78] p. 267.
8. Neter and Maynes [125] p. 503.

5

A Simultaneous Equation Problem: The Effect of Model upon the Econometric Estimators*

In the preceding chapter we have examined a single equation model where sampling experiments might be able to augment our information. This chapter presents the results of a pilot investigation of a problem with a simultaneous equation model. The principal impetus for this inquiry stems from the difference between the controlled environment, in which simultaneous equation estimators have been evaluated, and the one in which they must perform. Sampling (as well as analytical) evaluations of these techniques have in the past ignored the fundamental importance of the frame of reference for that evaluation. Quandt [131] has led the way in suggesting that such behavior cannot continue. Mosbaek and Wold [113] and Sasser [146] have followed his suggestion and begun such evaluations. This chapter reports upon a set of experiments explicitly tied to existing econometric models.

The first section of the chapter outlines in more detail the nature of the problem. Section 5.2 describes the three models used for our evaluation of three single-equation simultaneous estimators. In addition, it explicitly outlines the nature of experiments with each model. The third, fourth, and fifth sections of the chapter review the results with each model. In Section 5.6, some conjectural remarks are presented regarding the implications of model for the choice of an estimator. Finally, the last section summarizes the chapter.

5.1 A Statement of the Problem

The results of sampling experiments examining the small sample properties of simultaneous equation estimators (summarized in Chapter 3) indicate that there has been considerable diversity in the techniques' observed performance patterns. While there are a large number of design attributes which distinguish these studies, making comparison across them hazardous, one feature has been singled out as an important determinant of estimator performance. This characteristic is the model used to evaluate the techniques. As we noted in Chapter 3, Quandt [131] has conjectured that the magnitude of the bias in the estimates of the structural coefficients is a decreasing function of the sparseness (i.e., number of zeros) of the endogenous coefficient matrix. He argues that:

---

*The work reported in this chapter is based upon my dissertation [153], aspects of which have been reported in several papers—[154], [155] and [157].

Bias is caused by the fact that the Y's (endogenous variables) are all stochastic variables which, in turn, is due to the fact that they are jointly determined, given a specification of exogenous variables and error terms. The sparser the B (endogenous coefficient) matrix the likelier it is that the causal chains connecting the variables in the model contain no cycles. It seems plausible to argue that bias depends on how many causal feedbacks there are among the jointly determined variables.[1]

Sparseness must be measured in relative terms. Five zero elements in a four-equation model's endogenous coefficient matrix have different implications than the same number in a fourteen-equation system. Moreover, the positioning of the zero and nonzero elements is quite important. Consider an example. If we array a set of independent equations in matrix form, then the coefficient matrix for the endogenous variables (dependent in this case) will be an identity matrix. Alternatively, a recursive equation set is one in which the specific order of joint determination is specified and its endogenous coefficient matrix is triangular with all zero elements below (or above) the diagonal. In this case each endogenous variable is a stepping-stone in the chain of joint determination.

Most simultaneous equation models have coefficient arrays which do not follow simple recursive patterns.[a] Rather, the zero and nonzero elements are dispersed throughout the matrix. Thus, when alterations in the size and sparseness of the endogenous coefficient matrix are considered as determinants of estimator performance, an infinite number of possible arrays can be constructed. Accordingly, there is a need to discriminate between these possibilities in an analysis of the effects of model upon estimator performance.

Sasser [146] uses a measure of simultaneity derived from the fundamentals of graph theory. The measure is based upon the intensity of the simultaneous relations in all causal blocks in the model relative to the total possible.[2] His measure would be appropriate if all the effects of model size were reflected in the measure of simultaneity. However, as Mosbaek and Wold note, there are other model characteristics which are related to size and to estimator performance. It is these considerations which his measure does not reflect.[b] They found:

---

[a]Strotz and Wold [165] p. 417 have characterized recursive models as follows:

While triangularity of the coefficient matrix is a formal property of recursive models, the essential property is that each relation is provided a causal interpretation in the sense of a stimulus—response relationship.

Wold [178] p. 452 further notes that the distinction between simultaneous (his interdependent systems) and recursive (his causal chains) models as one of the nature of the inference:

We have seen that the parting of the ways between causal chains and interdependent systems lies at the level of explicit versus implicit inference from the behavior relations of the model. . . .

[b]Sasser [146] accounts for some of these other factors in his other determinants of estimator performance. See Chapter 3, Section 3.7.

The quality of estimates of coefficients in a model depends on the size of the model. There are, however, several ways in which size of a model may be measured. These include number of equations, number of structural (reduced form) coefficients, number of predetermined variables, and number of variables per equation. The various methods (DLS, FP, LSRF and 2SLS) are affected differently by increases in the model size as measured by each of the various measures.[3]

Their discussion should be amended somewhat when the concept of model simultaneity is considered. The model simultaneity is related to size, as are the number of equations, number of predetermined variables, degree of overidentification of each equation, number of variables in each equation, and number of structural coefficients. The problem of evaluating the effects of the model upon estimator performance is an intractable one if account must be taken of all variants of these factors. However, there is a simplification which allows some preliminary work to commence.

The essential point of the simplification is that the econometric estimators should be evaluated in a controlled environment which resembles the one within which they must perform. From a Bayesian viewpoint this scheme is synonymous with the selection of a prior distribution. With the sampling-theory point of view, this screening device reflects a specification of the long run set of conditions over which an estimator must perform well.[c] Monte Carlo research, in the past, has for the most part ignored the fundamental importance of the frame of reference to the estimator evaluation. Summers [166], in describing his model, best characterizes this attitude by stating that his model " . . . was deliberately made economically anonymous, with no direct real-life counterpart . . . so an appraisal of the estimating methods . . . would have general applicability."[4] The purpose of the research reported in this chapter has been to attempt a preliminary evaluation of the effects of the model upon estimator performance. A cross-section of existing macroeconometric models will be used to evaluate the estimators. This set consists of three models of varying size and sparseness. In addition, in order to avoid arbitrary decisions as to the true values of the structural coefficients and error variances, the specification of each will be made so as to replicate, as nearly as possible, the original estimating conditions.

When the models have been estimated with a variety of techniques, one set has been selected. Since the specification of the model does not change with other sets of coefficients, the numerical differences between the true values assigned to the structural coefficients are not great. Consequently, the selection of one of these several estimates will not have a decided impact upon the results.[d]

---

[c]Roberts [142] p. 26 makes this same point in relating the Bayesian approach to estimation to the classical view.

[d]See Cragg's [23] extensive study of coefficient value changes and their effect upon estimator performance.

The three models within which several estimating techniques will be
evaluated are linear structures ranging in size from six to thirty-four equations.
The first of these is an early macro model of the United States constructed by
Klein [81]. It is a six-equation model with three behavioral equations and three
identities.[5] The second model is also of the United States. It is a linearized
adaptation of the Klein–Goldberger [86] model which contains sixteen equations. It is derived from the Adelman and Adelman [1] version of the model. It
omits the tax equations and a nonlinear identity for the wage bill. There are
twelve behavioral relationships and four identities in the model as we have used
it.

The last model is a thirty-four equation model of Puerto Rico. The model
allows for free trade, free flow of capital, and the unrestricted population migra-
tion which the Puerto Rican economy enjoys with the United States. It contains
twenty-three stochastic equations and eleven identities. In both of Klein's models
extensive use is made of exact linear restrictions linking both exogenous and
endogenous variables, whereas in the Dutta–Su [39] model of Puerto Rico only
two instances of this form of restriction are observed.

Table 5.1 provides a more specific description of the structural characteristics of the models which are important to estimator performance. These
include the total number of equations, the percent of nonzero endogenous coefficients (i.e., sparseness), the number of stochastic equations, the number of
endogenous coefficients above and below the diagonal, the maximum number
of variables in the equations estimated, and the minimum degree of overidentification in these equations.

Several overall observations on the nature of the models are possible based
upon the comparative data in this table. (1) As the models increase in size the
sparseness, measured by the percent of coefficients in the endogenous coefficient matrix which are nonzero, tends to increase. (2) The distribution of nonzero coefficients above and below the diagonal in each of the three models is
approximately equal, so that none is any closer to a recursive structure. (3) The
minimum degree of overidentification increases with the size of the model.
Moreover, based upon Basmann's (8) conjecture, 2SLS is likely to possess finite
small sample moments up to at least the second order for all models. (4) The
percent of equations which are stochastic is largest with the Klein–Goldberger
model with approximately seventy-five percent of the equations as behavioral
relationships. The Dutta–Su model has a somewhat smaller percentage of
stochastic equations, with approximately sixty-eight percent, and finally the
Klein Model I has one-half of the model composed of stochastic relationships.

5.2 Design of the Experiments

Each of the models described above has been used to evaluate three single-
equation estimators. The techniques included are DLS (ordinary least squares

Table 5.1
A Comparison of the Models

Model	Total No. of Equations	Stochastic Equations	Percent Nonzero Coefficients	No. of Coefficients Above Diagonal	No. of Coefficients Below Diagonal	Maximum No. of Variables in Estimated Equation	Minimum Degree of Over-Identification[a]
Klein Model I	6	3	40	5	4	4	2b
Klein–Goldberger	16	12	19	15	18	7	20b
Dutta–Su	34	23	8	25	34	3	21

[a]If λ = the number of predetermined variables in the system, and k_j = number of estimated coefficients in the jth equation, then the degree of overidentification is $\lambda - k_j$. Basmann [8] has conjectured that 2SLS has finite moments up to this order. See Chapter 2, Section 2.3 for more discussion.
[b]These figures have been calculated under the assumption that the equations are estimated in unrestricted form. If we estimate the "combined" variables reflecting the restrictions, the minimum degree of overidentification increases to six for the Klein Model I and twenty-six for the Klein–Goldberger model.

on the structural form), 2SLS (two stage least squares), and LISE (limited information single equation maximum likelihood). Since the error covariance matrix for each of the three models has been postulated to be diagonal, the use of full information methods such as three stage least squares is uncalled for.[e]

The basic approach for each of the three models is similar. If we outline a general specification of a linear simultaneous equation system as in Equation (5.1), then the experiments can be easily described.

$$\beta\, Y_t + A\, Z_t + \sum_{i=1}^{R} C_i\, Y_{t-i} + U_t = 0 \qquad\qquad (5.1)$$

where:

β $= K \times K$ coefficient matrix for the endogenous variables

Y_t $= K \times 1$ vector of values for time t of the K endogenous variables

A $= K \times M$ coefficient matrix for the exogenous variables

Z_t $= M \times 1$ vector of values for time t of the M exogenous variables

C_i $= K \times K$ coefficient matrix for the ith lag of the K endogenous variables

Y_{t-1} $= K \times 1$ vector of the values for the ith lag of the K endogenous variables

U_t $= K \times 1$ vector of the values for time t of the K structural errors

Clearly, we have assumed that our model has K linear equations. It should be noted that identities in this framework have errors which are identically zero for all t. As we illustrated for a two-equation model, each Monte Carlo experiment requires specification of the true values for β, A, C_i, $i = 1, \ldots, R$, $(R =$ maximum lag), and the covariance matrix of U. Moreover, we need to be given a set of observations for the exogenous variables.

For each of the three models, we have used the original data series for the exogenous variables. Accordingly, these data sets constrain the sample size which may be used for our experiments. Both Klein's Model I and the Klein-

---

[e]There are several reasons for this restriction. One consideration is estimating large models with the system techniques. Klein [84] has done some work in this area, but in these cases there are insufficient degrees of freedom to estimate the two larger models. Moreover, the estimated error covariance structure based upon the Dutta–Su estimates of the Puerto Rico model is not of full rank and thus the generation of random deviates from a singular covariance structure becomes a problem. See Nagar [117] and McCarthy [105].

Goldberger model have twenty observations available. The Dutta–Su model was estimated with seventeen observations. For practical purposes the sample sizes are approximately equivalent in the three cases.

When this information is structured, then (5.1) is solved for the endogenous variables as a function of the predetermined variables and stochastic errors as in (5.2).

$$Y_t = -\beta^{-1} A Z_t - \beta^{-1} \sum_{i=1}^{R} C_i Y_{t-i} - \beta^{-1} U_t \qquad (5.2)$$

In order to simulate the model for each sample, it is necessary to generate the random errors (i.e., U_t) and provide a starting point for the lagged endogenous variables. In all three models, the errors are normal deviates generated from a multivariate parent distribution with zero mean vector and diagonal covariance matrix. The diagonal elements, the error variances, are selected to conform with the values estimated by the original author.[f] The objective for each experiment is to replicate, as nearly as possible, the original estimating conditions for each model. Thus, the starting values for the lagged endogenous variables are those reported by the original authors, and the generated values of endogenous variables, thereafter. Fifty samples have been generated for each model.

The Klein Model I is a six-equation model with consumption, (C), investment (I), and private wage bill (W_1) equations. Moreover, the identities define the capital stock (K), disposable income (DY), and profit (P). If we arrange the vectors Y_t and Z_t as follows, then the matrices in (5.1) are given in Equations (5.3) through (5.5).

$$Y_t = \begin{bmatrix} C_t \\ I_t \\ W_{1t} \\ K_t \\ P_t \\ DY_t \end{bmatrix} \qquad Z_t = \begin{bmatrix} 1 \\ G_t \\ t \\ T_{t-1} \\ W_{2t-1} \\ T_t \\ W_{2t} \end{bmatrix} \qquad Y_{t-1} = \begin{bmatrix} C_{t-1} \\ I_{t-1} \\ W_{1t-1} \\ K_{t-1} \\ P_{t-1} \\ DY_{t-1} \end{bmatrix}$$

---

[f]For the Klein Fluctuations Model I, the LISE estimates of the models were used to calculate the mean squared errors for the residuals. With the Klein–Goldberger model, the mean squared errors from the LISE model estimates' residuals were used. The model has been linearized according to the Adelman and Adelman procedure, consequently, these values probably understate what they would be in the actual linearized version of the model. Finally, with the Dutta–Su model, the specified error variances correspond to that estimated by the original authors. The true structural coefficients' values were specified to correspond to the LISE estimates given by Klein for Klein's Model I, the Adelman and Adelman values,

where:

G = government expenditures

t = time trend

T = taxes

W_2 = government wage bill

$$
\beta = \begin{bmatrix}
-1.0 & 0.0 & 0.87 & 0.0 & 0.02 & 0.0 \\
0.0 & -1.0 & 0.0 & 0.0 & 0.08 & 0.0 \\
0.0 & 0.0 & -1.0 & 0.0 & 0.0 & 0.43 \\
0.0 & 1.0 & 0.0 & -1.0 & 0.0 & 0.0 \\
0.0 & 0.0 & 1.0 & 0.0 & 1.0 & -1.0 \\
1.0 & 1.0 & 0.0 & 0.0 & 0.0 & -1.0
\end{bmatrix} \tag{5.3}
$$

$$
A = \begin{bmatrix}
17.72 & 0.0 & 0.0 & 0.0 & 0.0 & 0.0 & 0.87 \\
22.59 & 0.0 & 0.0 & 0.0 & 0.0 & 0.0 & 0.0 \\
1.53 & 0.0 & 0.13 & 0.15 & -0.15 & 0.43 & -0.43 \\
0.0 & 0.0 & 0.0 & 0.0 & 0.0 & 0.0 & 0.0 \\
0.0 & 0.0 & 0.0 & 0.0 & 0.0 & 0.0 & 1.0 \\
0.0 & 1.0 & 0.0 & 0.0 & 0.0 & -1.0 & 0.0
\end{bmatrix} \tag{5.4}
$$

$$
C_1 = \begin{bmatrix}
0.0 & 0.0 & 0.0 & 0.0 & 0.0 & 0.0 \\
0.0 & 0.0 & 0.0 & -0.17 & 0.68 & 0.0 \\
0.0 & 0.0 & 0.0 & 0.0 & 0.0 & 0.15 \\
0.0 & 0.0 & 0.0 & 1.0 & 0.0 & 0.0 \\
0.0 & 0.0 & 0.0 & 0.0 & 0.0 & 0.0 \\
0.0 & 0.0 & 0.0 & 0.0 & 0.0 & 0.0
\end{bmatrix} \tag{5.5}
$$

$$C_i = 0 \qquad i = 2, R$$

---

adapted, for the Klein–Goldberger model, and the ordinary least squares estimates for the Dutta–Su Model. For the specific values of each see Smith [153] pp. 54, 93, and 136.

Since the Klein–Goldberger and Dutta–Su models have large sparse coefficient matrices, these will not be presented in a format similar to the Klein Model I. Rather, the true values of the estimated coefficients will be presented when required.

The Klein–Goldberger model has been extensively discussed in the literature. Consequently, a detailed examination of the model is not necessary. Rather, we shall focus attention upon the characteristics which distinguish our linearized version of the model. First, the foreign sector is eliminated by assuming imports are always equal to exports. Second, the real farm income equation has been linearized. Third, interest rates are assumed constant. Finally, the investment equation has been respecified to be a function of current liquid assets held by households, to avoid singularity of the β matrix which occurred with this linearization and lagged liquid assets of households as the determinant of investment.[7] This model has several interesting features which distinguish it from both the Klein Model I and the Dutta–Su model. It contains the greatest number of lagged endogenous variables and also makes more extensive use of exact linear restrictions.[g] The original data series extends from 1929 to 1941 and 1946 to 1952. If the partitioning is appropriate (e.g., the periods represent "normal economic conditions"), then the generation of data should not "skip" these years, since the true structure does *not* accommodate the war years.

The Dutta–Su model of Puerto Rico, in contrast to the two previous models, has a highly developed foreign sector. It can be broken down into five sectors: consumption, investment, production, imports, and exports. Moreover, there is an equation for the wage bill. The six consumption equations are distinguished according to the type of good; food, services, nondurables, housing, automobiles, and other durables. Investment includes one exogenous component and two endogenous. Private investment, including both domestic and foreign, are determined by the model, while government investment expenditures are assumed exogenous.

The foreign sector encompasses the largest number of equations with eight import and three export equations. Imports are distinguished by the type of good; food, nondurable goods, automobiles, durable goods, capital goods, and raw materials, as well as outpayments. The payments made on the service account for Mainland investment as an approximate measure of "take home" profits of foreign investors and all other services round out the import side of the foreign sector.

Exports are divided into three categories including: services, traditional exports, and all other exports. Three linear stochastic production functions are

---

[g]Note that the effects of exact linear restrictions have all but been ignored in Monte Carlo studies. Klein and Goldberger suggest that the use of such restrictions improves the efficiency in estimation (pp. 46–48). My sampling results with the Klein Fluctuations Model I indicate that the root mean square errors of all coefficients, except the intercept of the consumption equation for all estimators, are larger in unrestricted forms than restricted. See Smith [155] pp. 41–42.

specified, with the output of agriculture the residual after subtracting from the total that of manufacturing and of other industries.

The application of DLS, 2SLS, and LISE to the Klein Fluctuations Model I is straightforward, since there are sufficient degrees of freedom to accommodate the latter estimators. In both the Klein–Goldberger and the Dutta–Su models, the number of predetermined variables exceeds the available sample size. Consequently, 2SLS and LISE may not be applied as theoretically formulated.[8] With the Klein–Goldberger model, the authors were confronted with the same problem. They discuss their resolution as follows:

> . . . it is desirable to choose a single set of predetermined variables applicable to the estimation of any equation in the system. An element of arbitrariness can be eliminated in this way. Because of restrictions on a system, it often happens that the number of predetermined variables explicitly occurring in any equation is less than the number of different predetermined variables in the system. In the model . . . we have used all explicitly occurring predetermined variables plus the most important among those remaining.[9]

The set of first stage regressors selected for 2SLS and LISE in our sampling experiments corresponds as closely as possible to those originally appearing. Table 5.2 provides an outline of the selections and the rationale for those omitted.

The original version of the Dutta–Su model was estimated with DLS and the authors did not confront this problem. Consequently, two versions of two-stage least squares and limited-information single-equation maximum-likelihood have been applied to the samples generated from this model. The first set with estimators designated 2SLS and LISE has as first stage regressors: population, government investment expenditures, other government expenditures, U.S. consumer expenditures on foreign travel, consumer expenditures on housing in the previous period, consumer expenditures on durables in the previous period, capital stock in the previous period, "take home" profits of foreigners in the previous period, imports of durables in the previous period, and net income of the previous period. The second set, whose estimators are 2SLS′ and LISE′, omits government investment expenditures and U.S. expenditures on foreign travel. The variables were selected on the basis of value judgments as to the important external influences upon the Puerto Rican economy.

Clearly, questions can be raised as to the comparability of 2SLS in the Klein Fluctuations Model I and its variants in the Klein–Goldberger and Dutta–Su models. However, two points should be recognized. The estimation of large models involves compromises of this character. The forms reported for these models may be more relevant to the practitioner, since they are based upon the kinds of decisions which must be made in estimating large-scale models. Additionally, it should be noted that consistency with 2SLS may be realized without the use of the complete set of predetermined variables in the first stage. It is this

Table 5.2
First Stage Predetermined Variables: A Comparison of
Klein–Goldberger Choice with Present Version

Variable in K–G Version	Current Decision	Reason for Omission
(1) Lagged consumer expenditures	Yes	
(2) Lagged liquid assets held by households	Yes	
(3) Population	Yes	
(4) Lagged disposable non-wage income plus depreciation and corporate saving	No	Duplication in factors contained in this variable with those in another included predetermined variable
(5) End of previous year capital stock	Yes	
(6) Lagged liquid assets held by enterprises	No	Omitted from investment equation, consequently omitted from first stage regressors, since L_{2t} equation not estimated
(7) Lagged price index for GNP (gross national product)	Yes	
(8) Two period lag of price index for GNP	Yes	
(9) Lagged corporate dividend payments	No	This variable does not appear in the present version of the model
(10) Lagged end-of-year accumulated corporate savings	Yes	
(11) Lagged GNP	Yes	
(12) Lagged imports of goods and services	No	This variable does not appear in the present version of the model
(13) Index of agricultural exports	No	This variable does not appear in the present version of the model
(14) Lagged deflated nonfarm disposable income	No	This variable does not appear in the present version of the model
(15) Government expenditures plus exports of goods and services	No	This variable does not appear in this form in the present model

property which is the primary advantage of 2SLS and it is a large sample property, whose relevance for small sample behavior is not clear.

5.3   Klein Fluctuations Model I—Sampling Results

As in the case of the single-equation Monte Carlo study, the results have been divided into two basic types—parametric and nonparametric measures of estimator performance. In the first case the three estimators are evaluated according to the criteria of bias, root mean squared error (RMSE), variance, and decentralization. The three stochastic equations for the model contain eleven structural coefficients. Table 5.3 summarizes the number of coefficients for each of three criteria that a given estimator performed best.

In terms of RMSE, bias, and variance 2SLS appears to be the best overall estimator of the consumption equation. This ranking is not as clear for either the investment or the wage equation. Table 5.4 presents the complete results for the investment equation. While decentralization is a problem with the coefficient of profit, it is even more acute for the coefficient of the same variable in the consumption equation, where LISE yields estimates with the wrong sign in thirty-six percent of the samples. 2SLS, for the same equation, does so in twenty-six percent of the cases, and DLS in only eight percent. In both cases the size of the true value of the coefficient is quite small relative to the other structural coefficients in each equation.

Another important feature of estimator performance is the consistency in the ranking of the estimators for each coefficient across the fifty samples. In Chapter 4 Kendall's coefficient of concordance was used to measure the percent agreement in the rankings of ordinary least squares with each Aitken estimator. For our present experiments, we shall compare the consistency in ranking of the three techniques together. Each set of estimates of the structural coefficients

Table 5.3
Summary Evaluation of the Estimators: Klein Model I[a]

	Criteria		
Estimator	*Bias*	*Variance*	*RMSE*
DLS	1	7	2½
2SLS	6	3½	7½
LISE	4	½	1
Total	11	11	11

[a]This table presents the number of coefficients which are estimated best with each method according to each of the three criteria. If a tie occurred each estimator was given the appropriate fraction. This table is reprinted with permission from "Economic Anonymity and Monte Carlo Studies," *Applied Economics,* Vol. 3, March 1971, p. 41.

Table 5.4
Parametric Results for the Investment Equation: Klein Model I[a]

Variable[b]	True Value	Estimating Technique	Decentralization[c]	Mean	RMSE	Bias	Var.
P_t	0.08	DLS	0.0	0.367	0.303	0.287	0.009
P_t	0.08	2SLS	0.08	0.271	0.247	0.191	0.025
P_t	0.08	LISE	0.22	0.095	0.246	0.015	0.061
P_{t-1}	0.68	DLS	0.0	0.483	0.222	-0.197	0.011
P_{t-1}	0.68	2SLS	0.0	0.553	0.195	-0.127	0.022
P_{t-1}	0.68	LISE	0.0	0.676	0.200	-0.004	0.040
K_{t-1}	-0.17	DLS	0.0	-0.140	0.058	0.030	0.003
K_{t-1}	-0.17	2SLS	0.0	-0.161	0.062	0.009	0.004
K_{t-1}	-0.17	LISE	0.0	-0.195	0.084	-0.025	0.006
Intercept	22.59	DLS	0.0	16.840	1.66	-5.750	69.285
Intercept	22.59	2SLS	0.0	20.533	1.98	-2.057	107.903
Intercept	22.59	LISE	0.0	26.737	1.88	4.147	184.925

[a]This table is based upon one reported in "Economic Anonymity and Monte Carlo Studies," *Applied Economics*, Vol. 3, March 1971, p. 40. It is reprinted with permission. One sample has been omitted because the LISE results were outliers.
[b]The variables are as defined in (5.2).
[c]Decentralization is the percent of samples with estimates with the wrong sign.

Table 5.5

Consistency in Estimator Rankings with Klein Fluctuations Model I: Coefficient of Concordance[a]

Equation	Structural Coefficient	True Value of Coefficient	Kendall's Coefficient of Concordance (w)[b]
Consumption	P_t	0.02	0.122**
	$(W_1 + W_2)_t$	0.87	0.051
	Intercept	17.72	0.104**
Investment	P_t	0.08	0.335**
	P_{t-1}	0.68	0.208**
	K_{t-1}	–0.17	0.040
	Intercept	22.59	0.045
Private Wage Bill	$(Y + T - W_2)_t$	0.43	0.037
	$(Y + T - W_2)_{t-1}$	0.15	0.050
	t	0.13	0.0006
	Intercept	1.53	0.018

[a]This table is based upon a similar one reported in "Economic Anonymity and Monte Carlo Studies," *Applied Economics*, Vol. 3, March 1971, p. 43. It is reprinted with permission.
[b]The critical values for a test (H_0: $w = 0$) may be estrapolated from Siegel [151].
**Significantly different from zero at 0.01 level.

was ranked according to the absolute proximity to the true value. Table 5.5 presents the results of this test. In the three equations, four of the eleven structural coefficients exhibit significant agreement in the estimator rankings across the fifty trials. In all of these four cases the single-equation simultaneous techniques are superior to DLS. Moreover, 2SLS is the best in three of the four cases. This test supports our overall findings with the model. In those cases where there is significant consistency in the estimator rankings, 2SLS appears to be the best technique.

Table 5.6

Summary Evaluation of the Estimators: Klein–Goldberger Model[a]

| Estimator | Criteria | | |
	Bias	Variance	RMSE
DLS	$12^1/_2$	$17^5/_6$	$17^1/_2$
2SLS	$2^1/_2$	$2^5/_6$	$3^1/_2$
LISE	6	$2/_6$	0
Total	21	21	21

[a]This table presents the number of coefficients which are estimated best with each method according to each of the three criteria. If a tie occurred each estimator was given the appropriate fraction.

Comparison of these results with previous studies (summarized in Chapter 3) indicates that there is a rough agreement. However, we did not find that both the single equation simultaneous estimators were superior to DLS, as most previous research would indicate. LISE was found to be generally inferior to DLS, while 2SLS was clearly better than both the other approaches. Cragg's [23] results indicate a fairly comparable performance pattern for 2SLS and LISE. However, LISE's performance has been shown to be erratic in several studies (e.g., Summers [166] and Sasser [146]), and given the recent analytical results concerning its finite sample moments (i.e., Mariano and Sawa [104]), these conclusions should not be overly surprising.

5.4 Klein–Goldberger Model–Sampling Results

Six of the twelve stochastic equations in this model have been estimated. They contain a total of twenty-one structural coefficients. As with the Klein Fluctuations Model I, both parametric and nonparametric statistics are used to evaluate the three estimators. The equations which were estimated include: consumption, corporate savings, capital consumption, corporate profits, private employee compensation, and liquid assets held by individuals.

Table 5.6 summarizes the overall performance of each technique with the twenty-one coefficients. There is clearly a marked distinction between the performance pattern of the estimators with the Klein–Goldberger model and that observed with the Klein Fluctuations Model I. In the present case DLS is uniformly the best technique using any of the three criteria of bias, variance, or RMSE, while in the Klein Fluctuations model 2SLS ranked best.

Rather than present each of the individual equation's results, we have chosen to present the results for one representative equation and then to "break down" the results in Table 5.6 on an equation by equation basis, reporting the best technique in each case individually. Table 5.7 presents the results for the consumption equation which contains the largest number of regressors of any equation in the model. It is representative of the behavior found with the other equations of the model, in most respects. However, for two parameters in other equations, decentralization was found to be a more severe problem than what is exhibited in the estimated coefficients for the consumption equation. For example, in estimating the effect of private GNP upon capital consumption, all the estimators provided estimates with the wrong sign in a large number of cases. DLS did so in forty-six percent of the samples, while 2SLS and LISE estimates had incorrect signs for fity-two and fifty-four percent of the cases, respectively. The true value of this coefficient was specified to be quite small (i.e., equal to 0.04), thus conforming to the experience with the Klein Fluctuations Model I. Severe decentralization was also experienced in estimating the intercept for the private employee compensation equation. With these exceptions, estimator per-

Table 5.7
Parametric Results for the Consumption Equation: Klein–Goldberger Model[a]

Variable[b]	True Value	Estimating Technique	Decentralization[c]	Mean	RMSE	Bias	Var.
$(w_1 + w_2 - T_w)_t$	0.55	DLS	0.0	0.543	0.055	-0.0075	0.0029
$(w_1 + w_2 - T_w)_t$	0.55	2SLS	0.0	0.542	0.065	-0.0077	0.0041
$(w_1 + w_2 - T_w)_t$	0.55	LISE	0.04	0.517	0.307	-0.0335	0.0929
$(P - T_p - S_p)_t$	0.41	DLS	0.0	0.423	0.046	0.0130	0.0020
$(P - T_p - S_p)_t$	0.41	2SLS	0.0	0.389	0.095	-0.0210	0.0087
$(P - T_p - S_p)_t$	0.41	LISE	0.02	0.428	0.472	0.0180	0.2220
$(A_1 + A_2 - T_a)_t$	0.34	DLS	0.0	0.355	0.036	0.0150	0.0011
$(A_1 + A_2 - T_a)_t$	0.34	2SLS	0.0	0.337	0.081	-0.0030	0.0065
$(A_1 + A_2 - T_a)_t$	0.34	LISE	0.02	0.401	0.268	0.0610	0.0681
C_{t-1}	0.26	DLS	0.0	0.261	0.047	0.0006	0.0022
C_{t-1}	0.26	2SLS	0.02	0.242	0.072	-0.0184	0.0049
C_{t-1}	0.26	LISE	0.02	0.299	0.295	0.0387	0.0856
L_{1t-1}	0.07	DLS	0.0	0.067	0.022	-0.0032	0.0005
L_{1t-1}	0.07	2SLS	0.0	0.072	0.021	0.0021	0.0004
L_{1t-1}	0.07	LISE	0.04	0.070	0.108	0.0004	0.0117
N_p	0.26	DLS	0.0	0.267	0.057	0.0065	0.0032
N_p	0.26	2SLS	0.0	0.298	0.109	0.0379	0.0104
N_p	0.26	LISE	0.06	0.243	0.408	-0.0173	0.1664
Intercept	-22.26	DLS	0.0	-22.936	4.252	-0.676	17.623
Intercept	-22.26	2SLS	0.0	-25.314	8.425	-3.054	61.654
Intercept	-22.26	LISE	0.04	-21.786	25.222	0.475	643.939

[a]Forty-six samples were used to estimate these results. Four samples were deleted as outliers.

[b]The symbols used in this table are defined as follows:

$w_1 + w_2 - T_w$ = disposable wage bill
$P - T_p - S_p$ = disposable nonwage, nonfarm income
$A_1 + A_2 - T_a$ = disposable farm income
C_{t-1} = lagged consumption expenditures
L_{1t-1} = lagged end-of-year liquid asset holdings of individuals
N_p = population

[c]Decentralization is the percent of samples with estimates with the wrong sign.

Table 5.8
Individual Equations' Results: Klein–Goldberger Model[a]

Equation	Criteria		
	Bias	Variance	RMSE
Consumption	DLS	DLS	DLS
Corporate Savings	DLS	DLS	DLS
Capital Consumption	DLS	DLS	DLS
Corporate Profits	DLS	DLS	DLS
Private Employee Compensation	LISE	DLS	DLS
Liquid Assets Held by by Individuals	LISE	2SLS	DLS

[a]This table reports the technique which estimated the majority of each equation's coefficients best under each of the three criteria.

formance for the remaining equations generally conforms to the behavior pattern of our example.

Table 5.8 summarizes the equation by equation results in more detail. Specifically, this table reports the estimator which performed best for the majority of the estimated coefficients in each equation under the criteria of bias, variance, and root mean squared error. Clearly, the results reinforce those of Table 5.6. DLS is the best technique for the majority of the estimated equations under any of the three criteria.

Table 5.9 reports the results of the test for consistency in the estimator rankings with Kendall's coefficient of concordance. Thirteen of the twenty-one estimated coefficients permit rejection of the hypothesis of no association. Thus, for the estimated coefficients, the performance patterns of DLS, 2SLS, and LISE appear to be more consistent over the fifty trials of this experiment than with the Klein Fluctuations Model I.

The findings of this experiment contrast with most Monte Carlo studies, since DLS, which is theoretically biased for simultaneous equation models, was found to be the best estimator. While Quandt's [131] comparisons of DLS and 2SLS indicate that there is not a clearcut ranking possible, they do not suggest as present findings do, that 2SLS and LISE, as applied here, are inferior to ordinary least squares estimates of the structural form.[10]

5.5 Dutta–Su Model–Sampling Results

The Dutta–Su and Klein–Goldberger models are the largest structures yet used for sampling experiments to evaluate the econometric estimators. Following the outline of the preceding two sections, we report a summary of the

Table 5.9

Consistency in Estimator Rankings with the Klein–Goldberger Model: Coefficient of Concordance

Equation	Structural Coefficient[a]	True Value of Coefficient	Coefficient of Concordance (w)[b]
Consumption	$(w_1 + w_2 - T_w)_t$	0.55	0.0410
	$(P - T_p - S_p)_t$	0.41	0.4590**
	$(A_1 + A_2 - T_a)_t$	0.34	0.1460**
	C_{t-1}	0.26	0.0510
	L_{1t-1}	0.07	0.1050*
	N_{pt}	0.26	0.1220**
	Intercept	-22.26	0.1620**
Corporate Savings	$(P_c - T_c)_t$	0.72	0.1570**
	B_{t-1}	-0.03	0.0060
	Intercept	-3.53	0.2550**
Capital Consumption	$(Y + T + D - w_2)_t$	0.04	0.3110**
	$(K_t + K_{t-1})$	0.05	0.0170
	Intercept	7.25	0.2480**
Corporate Profits	P_t	0.68	0.1680**
	Intercept	-7.60	0.2000**
Private Employee Compensation	$(Y + T + D - w_2)_t$	0.24	0.4130**
	$(Y + T + D - w_2)_{t-1}$	0.24	0.0510
	t	0.29	0.2040**
	Intercept	-1.40	0.0510
Liquid Assets Held by Individuals	$(w_1 + w_2 - T_w + P - T_p - S_p + A_1 + A_2 - T_a)_t$	0.14	0.0850
	Intercept	72.20	0.0450

[a] The variables used in this table are defined as follows:

$w_1 + w_2 - T_w$	=	disposable wage bill
$P - T_p - S_p$	=	disposable, nonwage, nonfarm income
$A_1 + A_2 - T_p$	=	disposable farm income
C_{t-1}	=	lagged consumption expenditures
L_{1t-1}	=	lagged end-of-year liquid assets holdings of individuals
N_p	=	population
$P_c - T_c$	=	disposable corporate profits
B_{t-1}	=	lagged end-of-year corporate surplus
$Y + T + D - w_2$	=	private gross national product
$K_t + K_{t-1}$	=	sum of lagged capital stock and current capital
P	=	nonwage, nonfarm income
t	=	time trend
$w_1 + w_2 - T_w + P - T_p - S_p + A_1 + A_2 - T_a$	=	disposable income

[b] The critical values for the test (H_0: w = 0) may be extrapolated from Siegel [151].

*Significantly different from zero at the 0.05 level.

**Significantly different from zero at the 0.01 level.

Table 5.10
Summary Evaluation of the Estimators: Dutta–Su Model[a]

| Equation | Criteria | | |
	Bias	Variance	RMSE
DLS	$13\frac{2}{3}$	$14\frac{29}{30}$	$17\frac{7}{10}$
2SLS	$2\frac{2}{3}$	$1\frac{29}{30}$	$2\frac{1}{5}$
LISE	$\frac{2}{3}$	$\frac{4}{5}$	$\frac{1}{5}$
2SLS'	6	$8\frac{29}{30}$	$6\frac{7}{10}$
LISE'	5	$1\frac{3}{10}$	$1\frac{1}{5}$
Total	28	28	28

[a]This table presents the number of coefficients which are estimated best with each method according to each of the three criteria. It is based upon a table in: "A Monte Carlo Experiment with a Large Macro-Econometric Model," *Western Economic Journal,* Vol. 8, December 1970, p. 380. The primary distinction is the omission of the results with the unrestricted inventory change equation.
[b]The distinction between 2SLS, LISE and 2SLS', LISE' is based upon the specification of the set of first stage regressors as noted earlier.

results for all the estimated equations of the Dutta–Su model,[h] the specific results for one example equation, and an equation by equation summary with parametric and nonparametric criteria. As with the Klein–Goldberger model, DLS ranked the best technique according to all criteria across all estimated coefficients. Table 5.10 reports a summary of the number of coefficients in the total of twenty-eight in which one technique performed better than the others according to each of the three criteria. The distinction between the two forms of 2SLS and LISE is not acute. It appears that 2SLS' performs slightly better than 2SLS and LISE' is approximately equivalent to LISE. Table 5.11 provides the parametric statistics for the imports of durables equation. It is representative of the other equations, since DLS is found to be the best estimator for the majority of its structural coefficients according to all criteria.[i]

In Table 5.12 the equation by equation evaluation is summarized and once again there is continued support for DLS as the most appropriate estimator for this model. The results do not seem as consistent as those exhibited with the Klein–Goldberger model. Nonetheless, all the evidence leads to the conclusion that DLS is again the most desirable approach for estimating the equations of this model.

The last component of the evaluation consists of an evaluation of the consistency in the estimator rankings across the fifty samples with each estimated coefficient. Table 5.13 reports the values of Kendall's coefficient of concordance

---

[h]Eleven of the twenty-three stochastic equations in the model were estimated, making a total of twenty-eight coefficients.

[i]The persistence of outliers with LISE resulted in discarding two samples for this equation. This finding conforms to results reported by both Summers [166] and Sasser [146]. Moreover, the recent analytical work by Mariano and Sawa [104], as noted in Chapter 2, provides some rationale for this erratic behavior.

Table 5.11
Parametric Results for the Imports of Durable Goods Equation: Dutta–Su Model[a]

Variable[b]	True Value	Estimating Technique	Decentralization[c]	Mean	RMSE	Bias	Var.
C_{dt}	0.25	DLS	0.0	0.263	0.046	0.013	0.0019
C_{dt}	0.25	2SLS	0.0	0.269	0.050	0.019	0.0021
C_{dt}	0.25	LISE	0.02	0.271	0.083	0.021	0.0064
C_{dt}	0.25	2SLS'	0.0	0.273	0.052	0.023	0.0020
C_{dt}	0.25	LISE'	0.02	0.268	0.142	0.018	0.0200
M_{dt-1}	0.37	DLS	0.0	0.332	0.146	-0.038	0.0200
M_{dt-1}	0.37	2SLS	0.0	0.314	0.157	-0.056	0.0220
M_{dt-1}	0.37	LISE	0.05	0.310	0.259	-0.060	0.0640
M_{dt-1}	0.37	2SLS'	0.02	0.299	0.164	-0.071	0.0220
M_{dt-1}	0.37	LISE'	0.06	0.316	0.453	-0.054	0.2030
Intercept	1.80	DLS	0.04	1.959	1.146	0.159	1.2880
Intercept	1.80	2SLS	0.04	2.028	1.190	0.228	1.3660
Intercept	1.80	LISE	0.10	1.995	1.500	0.195	2.2130
Intercept	1.80	2SLS'	0.02	2.155	1.130	0.355	1.1510
Intercept	1.80	LISE'	0.02	2.013	2.309	0.213	5.2880

[a]This table is based upon one reported in: "A Monte Carlo Experiment with a Large Macro-Econometric Model," *Western Economic Journal*, Vol. 8, December 1970, p. 381. It is reprinted with permission.

[b]The variables are defined as: C_{dt} = consumption of durable goods.
M_{dt-1} = lagged imports of durable goods.

[c]Decentralization is the percent of samples with estimated with the wrong sign.

Table 5.12
Individual Equations' Results: Dutta–Su Model[a]

	Criteria		
Equation	Bias	Variance	RMSE
Consumption			
Nondurables	TIE[b]	2SLS'	TIE[c]
Housing	DLS	DLS	DLS
Automobiles	DLS	2SLS'	DLS
Durables	DLS	DLS	DLS
Investment			
Private	LISE	2SLS'	2SLS'
Inventory Change	DLS	DLS	DLS
Imports			
Automobiles	LISE'	DLS	DLS
Nondurables	LISE'	2SLS'	2SLS'
Food	LISE'	DLS	2SLS
Durables	DLS	DLS	DLS
Raw Materials	2SLS	DLS	DLS

[a]This table is based upon one reported in "A Monte Carlo Experiment with a Large Macro-Econometric Model," *Western Economic Journal,* Vol. 8, December 1970, p. 381. It is reprinted with permission. The criterion for an estimator to be chosen as the best for a given equation is simply that it must have the smallest value of the relevant statistics for the majority of its structural coefficients.

[b]LISE' and 2SLS' are equally good under this criteria.

[c]DLS and 2SLS are equally good under this criteria.

for this model. These results indicate that thirteen of the twenty-eight structural coefficients exhibit significant agreement in the estimator rankings. In twelve of these thirteen cases DLS was the best technique according to the criteria of RMSE. Consequently, our results once again sharply contrast with the findings of most other Monte Carlo studies. In the next section of this chapter, we shall suggest some tentative explanations of this performance pattern.

5.6 Model Neutrality of the Estimators

The purpose of this chapter has been to commence an inquiry into the effect of the econometric model itself upon the performance of estimators. The results of our experiments must be interpreted cautiously for a number of reasons. They do *not* provide a test of the effects of the model upon estimating methods. However, they do lend strong support to the hypothesis that DLS, 2SLS, and LISE are not neutral with regard to the model. That is, each technique's performance is affected by the model within which it is evaluated.

Table 5.14 summarizes the results of earlier sections. In it we report the consistency of estimator rankings within each experiment, and for those co-

Table 5.13
Consistency in Estimator Rankings with the Dutta–Su Model:
Coefficient of Concordance[a]

Equation		Structural Coefficient[b]	True Value of Coefficient	Coefficient of Concordance (w)[c]
Consumption				
	Nondurables	Y_{pd}	0.288	0.0002
		Intercept	-15.300	0.0100
	Housing	Y_{pd}	0.030	0.0680
		C_{ht-1}	0.820	0.0280
		Intercept	-2.700	0.0100
	Automobiles	Y_{pd}	0.025	0.3280**
		C_{at-1}	0.720	0.2030**
		Intercept	-14.900	0.3100**
	Durables	Y_{pd}	0.830	0.3320**
		C_{dt-1}	0.490	0.3540**
		Intercept	-37.800	0.3950**
Investment				
	Private	M_{s2}	0.770	0.0420
		GP	0.120	0.0680*
		Intercept	-9.100	0.0130
	Inventory Change	$Y_t - Y_{t-1}$	0.350	0.1930*
		Intercept	1.000	0.440
Imports				
	Automobiles	C_a	0.580	0.0340
		Intercept	-1.900	0.0510
	Nondurables	C_{nd}	0.320	0.0050
		Intercept	6.900	0.0040
	Food	C_f	0.450	0.0170
		Intercept	-22.300	0.0004
	Durables	C_d	0.250	0.1770**
		M_{dt-1}	0.370	0.1720**
		Intercept	1.800	0.0210
	Raw Materials	Q_m	0.510	0.2370**
		Q_r	0.290	0.2530**
		Intercept	-45.200	0.2610**

[a]This table is based upon one reported in "A Monte Carlo Experiment with a Large Macro-Econometric Model," *Western Economic Journal,* Vol. 8, December 1970, p. 382

[b]The variables used in this table are defined as follows:

Y_{pd}	=	disposable income
C_{ht-1}	=	lagged consumption of housing
C_{at-1}	=	lagged consumption of automobiles
C_{dt-1}	=	lagged consumption of durables
M_{s2}	=	take-home profits of foreigners
GP	=	gross national product

$Y_t - Y_{t-1} =$ change in net income
C_{nd} = consumption of nondurables
C_f = consumption of food
C_d = consumption of durables
M_{dt-1} = lagged imports of durables
Q_m = gross product of manufacturing
Q_r = gross product of other industries

[c]The Kendall's coefficient has been calculated for DLS, 2SLS, and LISE omitting 2SLS' and LISE'. The critical values for the test (H_0: $w = 0$) may be extrapolated from Siegel [151].

*Significantly different from zero at the 0.05 level.

**Significantly different from zero at the 0.01 level.

efficients exhibiting consistent estimator rankings, the best technique using the RMSE criteria. The results completely confirm all our previous findings.

Direct least squares (i.e., ordinary least squares on the structural form) appears to be a more appropriate estimator for the two larger, more sparse models in our experiments. These results are suggestive of further hypotheses that DLS may be the best estimator of all larger, sparse econometric models. However, this statement is purely conjectural. A variety of other conditions, in addition to overall size and sparseness, have changed with the three experiments.

One of the most important of these alterations is the 2SLS and LISE estimators themselves. The degrees of freedom problem (i.e., the number of predetermined variables exceeds the available observations) has prevented application of these techniques as they were theoretically formulated. To the extent our adjustments are representative of other possibilities, we can still attribute the poor performance of 2SLS and LISE to the character of the models. That is, larger models will always require similar compromises and thus, comparisons of the theoretically correct 2SLS and LISE with DLS are not useful for most applications.

Since the research in this area is incomplete, our findings must remain

Table 5.14
Summary Evaluation for Coefficients with Consistent Rankings[a]

Model	Kendall's Coefficient of Concordance (w)		Number of Significant Rankings	Best Overall Technique
	Minimum	Maximum		
Klein Fluctuations Model I	0.0006	0.3350	4	2SLS
Klein–Goldberger	0.0060	0.4590	13	DLS
Dutta–Su	0.0002	0.3950	13	DLS

[a]This table is based upon one reported in "The Small Sample Properties of Selected Econometric Estimators in the Context of Alternative Macro Models," *Review of the International Statistical Association,* forthcoming.

suggestive rather than definitive. They do, however, find support in the more comprehensive investigation of Mosbaek and Wold [113]. These experiments also suggest that increases in model size improve DLS's performance relative to the single-equation simultaneous estimators. The notion that the frame of reference for estimator evaluation affects the outcome of such an appraisal should not be overly surprising. The diversity of findings of sampling experiments is in itself indicative that the frame of reference is of key importance. Our findings indicate the relative number of nonzero elements in the endogenous variables' coefficient matrix and their positioning influences performance of these techniques (DLS, 2SLS, and LISE).

5.7 Summary

This chapter has suggested one means of resolving the diversity of results with past Monte Carlo evaluations of the estimators for linear simultaneous equation systems. It consists in recognizing the importance of the model itself to the performance pattern of these techniques. Since a decision rule for estimator choice which implicitly assumes that they are neutral with regard to economic model would be of little value, systematic testing of the estimators within a rather diverse group of models seems essential. Briefly reviewing, we have suggested the following:

(1) The degree of simultaneity of a linear model, measured by the proportion of nonzero elements in the endogenous variables' coefficient matrix and their positioning, affects the performance of econometric estimators. The smaller the degree of simultaneity, the less necessary are the estimators which attempt to account for the joint determination.

(2) It is rather a "tall order" to evaluate the estimators within the context of an infinite number of models, so that some decision may be made as to the impact of the model upon each technique. Accordingly, recognizing the importance of the selection of a prior distribution to Bayesian analysis, we note that it is equally important to narrow the range of models by making reference to economically relevant models rather than anonymous ones.

(3) Three models—The Klein Fluctuations Model I, the Klein–Goldberger Model, and the Dutta–Su Model are selected for three experiments which constitute a *pilot* study of the effect of economic model upon estimator.

(4) The results for each experiment indicate that with the smallest model 2SLS is found to be the best estimator, while with the two larger models DLS is best. Generalizations beyond the present structures are hazardous. However, the evidence of Quandt [131] and Mosbaek and Wold [113] leads us to suggest that the DLS approach *may* be more appropriate for larger, sparser, macroeconometric models than are the single-equation simultaneous techniques (i.e., 2SLS and LISE) which we have examined.

Notes

1. Quandt [131] pp. 13–14. The parenthetical notes are added.
2. Sasser [146] pp. 63–66.
3. Mosbaek and Wold [113] pp. 377–378. The parenthetical note is added.
4. Summers [166] p. 4
5. Klein [81] pp. 58–80.
6. Dutta and Su [39].
7. Smith [153] pp. 87–88.
8. This problem is not an unusual one to econometrics. In fact, there is a fairly extensive literature on the subject including: Fisher [48], Mitchell [108], Mitchell and Fisher [109], Amemiya [2], McCarthy [106], and Kloek and Mennes [88].
9. Klein and Goldberger [86] p. 49.
10. See Quandt [131] p. 31.

6 Concluding Remarks

The purpose of this book was to explain the substance of Monte Carlo studies and to discuss their role for econometrics. The preceding five chapters have sought to describe the methodology, to compare it with the analytical approach, to review most of the published sampling experiments, and to discuss completely two case studies. The first of these was a single-equation problem, while the second involved a simultaneous-equation model.

The growth in the number of colleges and universities with large-scale computer facilities promises to generate a much greater volume of Monte Carlo research. In Chapter 1, we indicated that the Monte Carlo approach may also serve as a teaching aid, and therefore, it does not seem unreasonable to suggest that most students of econometrics will in all likelihood be exposed to simplified sampling experiments as a part of their basic curriculum. It is, therefore, important to stress, that it is well-defined problems in conjunction with careful experimental design and reasoned interpretation of results, which are the essential components of the Monte Carlo method and which ultimately distinguish it from " . . . high speed brute force computer groping . . .".[1]

It is equally important to note that a large portion of future research in the area will have to focus attention upon economically relevant problems. That is, the sampling experiment approach can be used to supplement the information already available as to the sensitivity of empirical findings and of estimator performance to the model's specification. Accordingly, rather than designing our experiments for broad applicability, many need to be tailored to specific problems. One early study which provides a good example of this approach is the evaluation of estimators for Cobb–Douglas production functions by Kmenta and Joseph [93].

Any list of the areas in which the focus of attention is on future sampling experiments would include the following:[2]

1.   Autocorrelation in simultaneous equation models.
2.   Nonlinear simultaneous equation models.
3.   Degrees of freedom problem in estimating large scale models.
4.   Nongaussian errors and econometric inference.
5.   Accounting for seasonal patterns.
6.   Iterative estimation versus traditional methods.

The list could be extended to fill several pages. However, the ultimate value of the future research using this approach will depend upon the extent to which the experiments are designed so that the results will compliment, supplement, and hopefully stimulate analytical results.

Notes

1.   Arnoff [5] p. 146.
2.   Research has begun in several of these areas. See Goldfeld and Quandt [57] and our review of sections of their monograph in Chapter 3.

Appendix A
Random Number Generation

Anyone who uses arithmetic methods of producing random digits is, of
course, in a state of sin (John Von Neumann, 1951)

The first step in constructing random variable generators is to design an algo-
rithm for the generation of pseudorandom numbers uniformly distributed over
the unit interval. While these numbers are produced from a completely deterministic formula by a digital computer, they satisfy the statistical properties of
an "idealized chance device" which selects numbers over the zero to one interval
independently will all values having equal likelihood of being selected.[a]

At present, despite some reservations in the computer science literature, the
most popular approach to generating these pseudorandom numbers is the multi-
plicative congruential method.[1] It produces long sequences of random digits and
requires little storage space. Given this sequence of numbers satisfying the
statistical prerequisites for that of a uniform (0, 1) random variable, the problem
remains to transform them so as to accommodate the distribution required for
each problem. For example, the problem may call for numbers from a uniform
distribution on the interval 10 to 45 rather than zero to one, or for numbers
from an exponential distribution.

In order to perform the transformation, it is necessary to understand the
relationship between a density function and a distribution function for continuous random variables, and a probability distribution and cumulative probability function for discrete variables. Consider an example of a discrete probability distribution given as follows:

$p(x)$	x	
0.25	2	
0.50	4	
0.25	6	(A.1)

where:

x = random variable

$p(x)$ = probability distribution function

---

[a]There are alternative procedures for generating random numbers, including mixed
congruential and the combination method.

Given (A.1), to derive the cumulative probability distribution it is necessary to determine the probability that $x \leqslant c$ where c is a constant which takes on values of 2, 4, and 6 in this case. Consequently, the cumulative probability distribution may be written as in (A.2).

$$
\begin{array}{cc}
\text{Prob. } (x \leqslant c) & c \\
0.25 & 2 \\
0.75 & 4 \\
1.00 & 6
\end{array}
\tag{A.2}
$$

With (A.2) and a random number generator providing numbers from a $(0, 1)$ uniform distribution it is possible to generate pseudorandom numbers from (A.1). For example, suppose that the uniform generator provides a value of 0.66, the value of x which should correspond is 4. The reasoning is straightforward. The probability distribution in (A.1) indicates that twenty-five percent of the time the "process" yields a value of 2, fifty percent of the time 4, and twenty-five percent a value of 6. Since our uniform generator produces a sequence of numbers from the interval 0 to 1 each one with equal likelihood, then twenty-five percent of the time it will provide values between 0 and 0.25, fifty percent of the time values between 0.25 and 0.75, and twenty-five percent of the time values between 0.75 and 1.00. Thus, when a value of the uniform falls within one of these intervals, we assign to x a value corresponding to 2, 4, or 6 as (A.2) indicates.

The Bernoulli random variable used in the experiments in Chapter 4 is a good example. Recall that the probability distribution of the error structure assumed for this model was described as follows:

$$
\text{Prob } (u_i = -x_i\beta) = 1 - x_i\beta
$$

$$
\text{Prob } (u_i = 1 - x_i\beta) = x_i\beta
\tag{A.3}
$$

where:

$x_i = 1 \times K$ vector of regressors

$\beta_i = K \times 1$ vector of parameter values

Since this is a two-valued random variable for each x_i, it is straightforward to transform from the uniform $(0, 1)$ to that of (A.3). $1 - x_i\beta$ percent of the time the values must be $- x_i\beta$ and $x_i\beta$ percent of the time the values must be $1 - x_i\beta$. Thus, if the uniform generator provides a value less than or equal to $1 - x_i\beta$, U_i is $- x_i\beta$, otherwise U_i is $1 - x_i\beta$.

For continuous random variables the procedure is conceptually similar, but in practice there may need to be some alterations. First, the distribution function for a continuous random variable is usually defined as a function which indicates the probability that the random variable in quesion is less than or equal to some constant, c, for all real c. The density function is that function which describes the slope of the distribution function $F(x)$ (i.e., density $= dF(X)/dx)^2$ The range for the distribution function is from zero to one.

If it is possible to solve for c (the constant) in terms of $F(x)$, then a straightforward approach to generation of continuous pseudorandom numbers is the inverse transformation method. In order to appreciate the procedure, consider an example—a random variable, V, uniformly distributed on the interval from 10 to 45. The density function, $f(v)$, for V is given in (A.4).

$$f(v) = \begin{cases} \dfrac{1}{35} & 10 < v < 45 \\ 0 & \text{otherwise} \end{cases} \tag{A.4}$$

The distribution function is given as the integral of $f(v)$ from minus infinity to c, the value of interest. Equation (A.5) describes it.

$$F(c) = \int_{-\infty}^{c} f(v)\, dv = \int_{10}^{c} \frac{1}{35}\, dv$$

$$F(c) = \frac{c - 10}{35} \tag{A.5}$$

Solving for c we have (A.6).

$$c = 35F(c) + 10 \tag{A.6}$$

Since our uniform (0, 1) generator provides values on the zero to one interval with equal likelihood, we may substitute these values for $F(c)$ in (A.6), and the corresponding c's will follow a uniform distribution on the interval 10 to 45, as we required.

Consider another example, the exponential distribution (i.e., $f(v) = \beta\, e^{-\beta v}$ for $\beta > 0$ and $v \geqslant 0$). Equation (A.7) provides the distribution function.

$$F(c) = \int_{-\infty}^{c} \beta e^{-\beta v}\, dv = \int_{0}^{c} \beta e^{-\beta v}\, dv$$

$$F(c) = -e^{-\beta v}\big]_{0}^{c}$$

$$F(c) = 1 - e^{-\beta c} \tag{A.7}$$

Solving for c we have (A.8).

$$c = -\frac{1}{\beta} \ln (1 - F(c))$$ (A.8)

Substituting the generated values on the $(0, 1)$ interval for $F(c)$, we have a sequence of c's from an exponential distribution.

Since the normal distribution's distribution function cannot be "inverted" analytically (i.e., we cannot solve for c in terms of $F(c)$), several approaches have evolved. The first makes use of the central limit theorem which suggests that the distribution of sample means approaches normality when the size of the sample increases and the observations are selected from distributions with finite first and second moments. The others consist of approximations to an inverse for the normal distribution (see Schmidt and Taylor [149]). The normal distribution is not the only case in which generators are derived by other than the inverse transformation of the distribution function. For example, a standardized Cauchy random variable may be produced by taking the ratio of two independent standardized normal variables.

This appendix has sought to review, very briefly, the considerations underlying random number generators. Before any newly constructed generator is used it should be subjected to the statistical tests available to discern whether or not the sequence of generated values is significantly different from that produced by a truly random process.[3]

Notes

1. See Naylor [119] and Naylor, Balintfy, Burdick and Chu [120] for further details.
2. See Brunk [14] for a more detailed and rigorous description.
3. See Naylor, Balintfy, Burdick and Chu [120] and Schmidt and Taylor [149].

Appendix B
Test Statistics: Parametric and Nonparametric

In order to discriminate between estimators, it is necessary to define a loss function which assesses those characteristics of a technique's performance pattern which are the most important. However, loss functions will differ according to the use to which a technique is put. Consequently, sampling studies usually present a variety of descriptive statistics for each estimator and leave the definition of specific loss functions to those who wish to use their findings.

The parametric statistics are those measures of estimator performance which have a distribution, while nonparametric are distribution-free. Several important measures of estimator properties are the bias, variance, and root mean squared error. The bias is defined to be the difference between the mean of the sample of estimates for a given experiment and the true value of the parameter of interest. Equation (B.1) presents the definition mathematically.

$$\text{Bias} = \frac{1}{n} \sum_{i=1}^{n} \hat{\beta}_i - \beta \tag{B.1}$$

where:

$\hat{\beta}_i$ = estimate of β

β = true value of parameter

n = sample size

An unbiased estimator is one which is, on average, right on target (i.e., $E(\hat{\beta}) = \beta$). The variance of the estimates is the mean sum of squared deviations of the estimates about their mean and is given in (B.2).

$$\text{Var} = \frac{1}{n} \sum_{i=1}^{n} (\hat{\beta}_i - \bar{\hat{\beta}}_i)^2 \tag{B.2}$$

This is one measure of the dispersion of the estimator's distribution. If we are to make use of it, we should be sure that the estimator in question has a finite second moment. The root mean squared error is the square root of the variance of the estimates about the true value of the parameter (i.e., the square root of the mean squared error), and is defined in (B.3).

$$\text{RMSE} = \sqrt{\frac{1}{n} \sum_{i=1}^{n} (\hat{\beta}_i - \beta)^2}$$
(B.3)

The mean squared error can be shown to be the sum of variance and bias squared. Once again, meaningful interpretation of these statistics requires that their theoretical counterparts exist. That is, both the variance and mean squared error are measures of the dispersion in the distribution for a particular estimator of a given parameter. If the distribution does not have a finite second moment, then as we noted in Chapter 2, the value of these statistics is questionable.

Another possible measure is the mean sum of absolute deviations (MSAD). If we are concerned with how close on average (without regard to direction) we are to the true value of the parameter, this represents a perfectly rational measure of estimator performance. It is given in (B.4).

$$\text{MSAD} = \frac{1}{n} \sum_{i=1}^{n} |\hat{\beta}_i - \beta|$$
(B.4)

There are a variety of other measures which might be used to provide an indication of the dispersion in an estimator's sampling distribution. One of the more popular is the interquartile range. This measure gives the length of the interval containing the middle fifty percent of the parameter estimates. Unlike the range, this measure is not affected by one or two outliers in the estimates.

In addition to measures of the dispersion in an estimator's sampling distribution, the central tendency is also of substantial importance. The preceding measures have assumed that the arithmetic mean was our desired measure. The median (i.e., value which divides the distribution in half) is also frequently presented, since this measure will always exist even if the distribution has no finite moments of any order. If the concern is for frequent extreme errors, Quandt [131] suggests that a measure of decentralization is required. One measure of this property is the percent of the samples in which the parameter estimates have the wrong sign.

It was noted in the first chapter that since each estimator is applied to the same set of samples, the corresponding estimates are not independent across techniques. Consequently, estimator comparisons are usually made with nonparametric statistics. The assumptions underlying more traditional parametric test statistics are not likely to be upheld. There are a wide array of such tests which can be found in Siegel [151] and Conover [20]. We shall discuss three such statistics—Spearman's rank correlation coefficient, Kendall's coefficient of concordance, and the Wilcoxon signed ranks matched pairs test.

The Spearman rho (ρ) measures the association between two ordinally-scaled variables. It is given by (B.5). The variables x and y are the values of the ranks for the same set of samples. Suppose for example we wanted to compare the ranking of seven estimators according to absolute bias with that according to variance. First, we would rank each technique according to each criteria, then we would have two sets of seven ranked observations each. These are our x and y.[a]

$$\rho = 1 - 6 \, \frac{\sum\limits_{i=1}^{N} d_i}{N^3 - N} \tag{B.5}$$

where:

$$d_i = x_i - y_i$$

N = number of ranked items

Kendall's coefficient of concordance (w) provides a measure of the relationship among *several* rankings, rather than two as with the Spearman's rho. In fact, it is a linear function of the average of the Spearman rank correlation coefficients between the rankings of all possible pairs of the items. This coefficient is an index of the divergence of the actual agreement shown in the data from the maximum possible agreement. Equation (B.6) presents the procedure for its calculation.

$$w = \frac{s^2}{1/12 \, K^2 \, (N^3 - N)} \tag{B.6}$$

where:

s^2 = sum of squared observed deviations from mean sum of ranks

---

[a] Siegel [151] pp. 206–208 presents a correction for ties. They are assigned the average of the ranks which would have been assigned in the absence of ties. When the proportion of ties is large, a correction factor must be incorporated into the computational process.

K = the number of sets of rankings

N = the number of entities ranked

$1/12 \cdot K^2 (N^3 - N)$ = maximum possible sum of squared deviations

s^2 $= \displaystyle\sum_{j=1}^{N} \sum_{i=1}^{K} (R_{ij} - \bar{R})^2$

R_{ij} = rank of the jth estimator for i^{th} sample

$\bar{R}$ $= \dfrac{\displaystyle\sum_{j=1}^{N} \sum_{i=1}^{K} R_{ij}}{N}$

Both of the preceding tests suffer from the disadvantage that they do not take account of the magnitude of the discrepancies between estimator performance. That is, we do not account for how much better or worse one technique is relative to another. The Wilcoxon matched-pairs signed-ranks test allows account to be taken of both the direction of differences and their magnitude in pair-wise comparisons. Thus, it gives more weight to a pair that shows a large difference than one which shows a small one.

This test is calculated by examining a pair of estimator's absolute bias for each of the experiments that comprise the model (say ten for example). These values are then subtracted and the resulting differences ranked by absolute magnitude. If the difference was positive, the corresponding rank is given a plus sign, while if the difference was negative, it is assigned a minus. If the estimators' performance patterns, measured by absolute bias, are equivalent across experiments, we would expect the rank sum of the plus ranks to be approximately equal to the rank sum from the minus. Tables have been constructed so that the null hypothesis of no difference might be tested.

In addition to the above tests, there are a variety of other nonparametric tests which are useful to specific problems which need to be evaluated within the context of a series of sampling experiments. Moreover, frequently the design of the experiments permits the application of parametric test statistics (see Schink and Chiu [148] and Sasser [146]).

Appendix C
A Brief Review of Econometric Estimators

The purpose of this appendix is to explain, as simply as possible, some of the estimators referred to in Chapters 3 and 5 for linear simultaneous equation models. Since there are a large number of excellent textbooks available in econometrics, a comprehensive treatment of the techniques will not be attempted. Rather, the objective is to discuss in the context of a simple two-equation model, several of the econometric estimators.

Assume the model to be estimated is given in Equations (C.1) and (C.2) and there are T observations available for the purposes of estimation (with $T > 4$).

$$y_{1t} = \gamma_{10} + \gamma_{11} Z_{1t} + \beta_{12} y_{2t} + u_{1t} \tag{C.1}$$

$$y_{2t} = \gamma_{20} + \gamma_{22} Z_{2t} + \gamma_{23} Z_{3t} + \beta_{21} y_{1t} + u_{2t} \tag{C.2}$$

where:

y_{it} = endogenous variable

Z_{it} = predetermined variable

u_{it} = structural error

The first equation of the model is overidentified, since the number of excluded predetermined variables exceeds the number of included endogenous variables less one. The second equation is exactly identified.

Ordinary least squares estimation of the structural model (designated direct least squares in Chapters 3 and 5) estimates each equation individually. The parameter estimates are selected so as to minimize the sum of squared residuals for each equation (i.e., choose γ_{10}, γ_{11} and β_{12} so that

$$\sum_{t=1}^{T} (y_{1t} - \gamma_{10} - \gamma_{11} Z_{1t} - \beta_{12} y_{2t})^2$$

is a minimum). Since y_{2t} does not satisfy the properties of a regressor as they are described in the classical linear model, both single-equation and system estimators have been proposed to account for the simultaneity problems. The instrumental variables method suggests that we define a variable or set of variables which are closely related to the right-hand side endogenous variable (s), yet which satisfy the assumptions of the general linear model, and use them as illustrated with estimation of (C.1).[a] Equation (C.3) presents the instrumental variable estimator with w_t as the instrument for y_{2t}.

$$
\begin{bmatrix} \gamma_{10} \\ \gamma_{11} \\ \beta_{12} \end{bmatrix}_{IV} = \begin{bmatrix} T & \Sigma Z_{1t} & \Sigma y_{2t} \\ \Sigma Z_{1t} & \Sigma Z_1{}^2{}_t & \Sigma Z_{1t} y_{2t} \\ \Sigma w_t & \Sigma w_t Z_{1t} & \Sigma w_t y_{2t} \end{bmatrix}^{-1} \begin{bmatrix} \Sigma y_{1t} \\ \Sigma Z_{1t} y_{1t} \\ \Sigma w_t y_{1t} \end{bmatrix} \quad (C.3)
$$

The instruments may be constructed in a variety of ways. One recent iterative scheme, the iterative instrumental variables method, uses the forecasts from the ordinary least squares estimates of the restricted reduced form first, and the predictions from successive parameter estimates until convergence is achieved.[1] Brundy and Jorgenson [13] have suggested that this process need not be carried out to convergence. They note that:

> . . . the third stage in their (Dutta and Lyttkens [37]) iterative process, the second instrumental variables estimator is asymptotically equivalent to a two-stage least squares estimator.[2]

However, some preliminary small-sample studies indicated that the iterative instrumental variable approach has a performance pattern more comparable to three-stage least squares than to other single equation simultaneous techniques.[3]

Another approach to the estimation of equations from linear simultaneous equation systems is two-stage least squares. Dhrymes [31] has characterized this approach as an optimal instrumental estimator for a particular class of models.[4] The estimator is conceptually appealing. Each right-hand side endogenous variable is regressed upon all the predetermined variables in the system, and then the predictions from these unrestricted reduced form equations are used in ordinary least squares regressions. Thus equation (C.4) provides the two-stage estimator.[b]

$$
\begin{bmatrix} \gamma_{10} \\ \gamma_{11} \\ \beta_{12} \end{bmatrix}_{2SLS} = \begin{bmatrix} T & \Sigma Z_{1t} & \Sigma \hat{y}_{2t} \\ \Sigma Z_{1t} & \Sigma Z_1{}^2{}_t & \Sigma Z_{1t} \hat{y}_{2t} \\ \Sigma \hat{y}_{2t} & \Sigma \hat{y}_{2t} Z_{1t} & \Sigma \hat{y}_{2t}^2 \end{bmatrix}^{-1} \begin{bmatrix} \Sigma y_{1t} \\ \Sigma Z_{1t} y_{1t} \\ \Sigma \hat{y}_{2t} y_{1t} \end{bmatrix} \quad (C.4)
$$

[a]These assumptions are reviewed in Chapter 2.

[b]We have assumed that the number of observations is greater than the number of predetermined variables in the model. The recent literature suggests a variety of alternatives when this is not the case. See McCarthy [106], Kloek and Mennes [88], Brundy and Jorgenson [13], Mitchell and Fisher [109].

where:

$$\hat{y}_{2t} = \hat{\pi}_0 + \hat{\pi}_1 Z_{1t} + \hat{\pi}_2 Z_{2t} + \hat{\pi}_3 Z_{3t}$$

$$\hat{\pi}_0, \hat{\pi}_1, \hat{\pi}_2, \hat{\pi}_3 = \text{ordinary least squares estimates}$$

The Theil-Nagar k-class estimators can be written in (C.5). k is a scalar which may be determined to satisfy certain predetermined criteria (see Nagar [115]). If $k = 1$, then the k-class becomes two stage least squares, and if $k = 0$, the estimator is direct least squares.

$$
\begin{bmatrix} \gamma_0 \\ \gamma_{11} \\ \beta_{12} \end{bmatrix}_{k\text{-class}}
=
\begin{bmatrix}
T & \Sigma Z_{1t} & \Sigma y_{2t} \\
\Sigma Z_{1t} & \Sigma Z_1^2{}_t & \Sigma Z_{1t} y_{2t} \\
\Sigma y_{2t} & \Sigma y_{2t} Z_{1t} & \Sigma y_{2t}^2 - k\Sigma v_t^2
\end{bmatrix}^{-1}
\begin{bmatrix}
\Sigma y_{1t} \\
\Sigma Z_{1t} y_{1t} \\
\Sigma y_{2t} y_{1t} - k\Sigma v_t y_{1t}
\end{bmatrix}
$$

with   (C.5)

$$\hat{v}_t = \text{residuals from the ordinary least squares estimates of the unrestricted reduced form}$$

One special member of this class is the limited-information maximum-likelihood estimator where k is given by the smallest root of the determinantal equation in (C.6).

$$
\det
\begin{bmatrix}
\Sigma \bar{v}_1^2{}_t - \lambda \Sigma \hat{v}_t^{*2} & \Sigma \bar{v}_{1t} \bar{v}_{2t} - \lambda \Sigma \hat{v}_t^* \hat{v}_t \\
\Sigma \bar{v}_{2t} \bar{v}_{1t} - \lambda \Sigma \hat{v}_t \hat{v}_t^* & \Sigma \bar{v}_2^2{}_t - \lambda \Sigma \hat{v}_t^2
\end{bmatrix}
= 0
$$

(C.6)

where:

$$\bar{v}_{1t} = \text{residuals from regression of } y_{1t} \text{ on } Z_{1t}$$

$$\bar{v}_{2t} = \text{residuals from a regression of } y_{2t} \text{ on } Z_{1t}$$

$$\hat{v}_t = \text{residuals from a regression of } y_{2t} \text{ on } Z_{1t}, Z_{2t}, Z_{3t}$$

$$\hat{v}_t^* = \text{residuals from a regression of } y_{1t} \text{ on } Z_{1t}, Z_{2t}, Z_{3t}$$

It should be noted that the limited-information maximum-likelihood (least variance ratio) estimator is invariant with normalization rule, while two-stage least squares is not.[5] This property is offset by the exact small-sample finding of

Mariano and Sawa [104] that no finite moments of any order exist for the estimator with a reasonably general model.

If we rewrite the model in (C.1) and (C.2), it is possible to describe three-stage least squares as an Aitken generalized estimator. (C.7) presents the compact form of the system.

$$
\begin{bmatrix} y_{1t} \\ y_{2t} \end{bmatrix} = \begin{bmatrix} 1 & Z_{1t} & y_{2t} & 0 & 0 & 0 & 0 \\ 0 & 0 & 0 & Z_{2t} & Z_{3t} & y_{1t} & 1 \end{bmatrix} \begin{bmatrix} \gamma_{10} \\ \gamma_{11} \\ \beta_{12} \\ \gamma_{22} \\ \gamma_{23} \\ \beta_{21} \\ \gamma_{20} \end{bmatrix} + \begin{bmatrix} u_{1t} \\ u_{2t} \end{bmatrix} \qquad \text{(C.7)}
$$

Replacing these variables by vectors containing the T observations on each component of the model, we can write (C.7) as (C.8)

$$
Y = X\bar{\alpha} + U \qquad \text{(C.8)}
$$

with

$Y \ = \ 2T \times 1$ vector

$X \ = \ 2T \times 7$ matrix

$U \ = \ 2T \times 1$ vector

Replacing the right-hand side endogenous variables in (C.8) by their unrestricted reduced form predictions, we can write the three-stage least squares estimates of $\bar{\alpha}$ as:

$$
\begin{bmatrix} \gamma_{10} \\ \gamma_{11} \\ \beta_{12} \\ \gamma_{22} \\ \gamma_{23} \\ \beta_{21} \\ \gamma_{20} \end{bmatrix}_{3SLS} = (\hat{X}^T \hat{\Sigma}^{-1} \hat{X})^{-1} (\hat{X}^T \hat{\Sigma}^{-1} Y)
\qquad\qquad (C.9)
$$

with

$\hat{\Sigma}$ = two-stage least squares estimates of the following matrix:

$$
\begin{bmatrix} \text{Var } (u_1) & \text{Cov } (u_1 u_2) \\ \text{Cov } (u_1 u_2) & \text{Var} (u_2) \end{bmatrix} \otimes I
$$

The full-information maximum-likelihood estimates of the structural coefficients are derived by maximizing the log likelihood function for the whole system. Further discussion of this technique will not be presented at this point. The interested reader is referred to a variety of texts (i.e., Dhrymes [31] pp. 316–328, Kmenta [90] pp. 578–581, and Theil [170] pp. 524–526).

The last technique which will be reviewed is the fixed point method derived by Wold [179]. It suggests an ordinary least squares regression of the equations (C.1) and (C.2) using different linear combinations of the predetermined variables for each of the right-hand side endogenous variables. Then these estimates, denoted with a "hat" ($\hat{\ }$), are used for single-equation prediction of each left-hand side endogenous variable. These predictions are in turn used in direct least squares (i.e., ordinary least squares on the structural equations) of the structural equations.

$$
y^i_{1t} = \hat{\gamma}_{10}{}^i + \hat{\gamma}_{11}{}^i Z_{1t} + \hat{\beta}_{12}{}^i y_{2t}{}^{(i-1)}
\qquad\qquad (C.10)
$$

$$
y^i_{2t} = \hat{\gamma}_{20}{}^i + \hat{\gamma}_{22}{}^i Z_{2t} + \hat{\gamma}_{23}{}^i Z_{3t} + \hat{\beta}_{21}{}^i y_{1t}{}^{(i-1)}
\qquad\qquad (C.11)
$$

The superscript denotes the iteration step in Equations (C.10) and (C.11), which provide the means of calculating the values to be used for the $i + 1$ direct least squares estimates.

This process is continued until a preassigned convergence criteria is satisfied. Mosbaek and Wold [113] note that convergence is an important hazard with this approach. Moreover, Maddala [100] in algebraic solutions with Summers' model, also finds it to be a serious consideration.

Notes

1.   See Dutta and Lyttkens [37].
2.   Brundy and Jorgenson [13] p. 212 (note).
3.   See Dutta, Smith and Loeb [38].
4.   See Dhrymes [31] pp. 184–185.
5.   See Goldberger [54] pp. 424–431.

References

1. Adelman, I. and Adelman, F.L. "The Dynamic Properties of the Klein–Goldberger Model." *Econometrica,* Vol. XXVIII, October, 1959.
2. Amemiya, T. "On the Use of Principal Components of Independent Variables in Two-Stage Least Squares Estimation." *International Economic Review,* Vol. VII, September, 1966.
3. ——. "Specification Analysis in the Estimation of Parameters of a Simultaneous Equation Model With Autoregressive Residuals." *Econometrica,* Vol. XXXIV, 1966.
4. —— and Fuller, W. "A Comparative Study of Alternative Estimators in a Distributed Lag Model." *Econometrica,* Vol. XXXV, July–October, 1967.
5. Arnoff, Leonard. "Successful Models I Have Known." *Decision Sciences,* Vol. II, April, 1971.
6. Ashar, V.G. and Wallace, T.D. "A Sampling Study of Minimum Absolute Deviations Estimators." *Operations Research,* Vol. XI, 1963.
7. Basmann, R.L. "A Note on the Exact Finite Sample Frequency Functions of Generalized Classical Linear Estimators in Two Leading Over-Identified Cases." *Journal of the American Statistical Association,* Vol. LVI, September, 1961.
8. ——. "A Note on the Exact Finite Sample Frequency Functions of Generalized Classical Linear Estimators in a Leading Three Equation Case." *Journal of the American Statistical Association,* Vol. LVIII, March, 1963.
9. ——. "The Causal Interpretation of Non-Triangular Systems of Economic Relations." *Econometrica,* Vol. XXXI, July, 1963.
10. ——, Brown, F.L., Dawes, W.S., and Schoepfle, G.K. "Exact Finite Sample Density Functions of GCL Estimators of Structural Coefficients in a Leading Exactly Identifiable Case." *Journal of the American Statistical Association,* Vol. LXVI, March, 1971.
11. Bergstron, A.R. "The Exact Sampling of Least Squares and Maximum Likelihood Estimators of the Marginal Propensity to Consume." *Econometrica,* Vol. XXX, 1962.
12. Blattberg, R., and Sargent, T. "Regression with Non-Gaussian Stable Disturbances: Some Sampling Results." *Econometrica,* Vol. XXXIX, May, 1971.
13. Brundy, J.M. and Jorgenson, D.W. "Efficient Estimation of Simultaneous Equations By Instrumental Variables." *Review of Economics and Statistics,* Vol. LIII, August, 1971.
14. Brunk, H.D. *An Introduction to Mathematical Statistics.* (Waltham, Mass: Blaisdell Publishing Co: 1965).
15. Chow, G.C. "A Comparison of Alternative Estimators for Simultaneous Equations." *Econometrica,* Vol. XXXII, October, 1964.

16. Christ, C.F. "Simultaneous Equation Estimation: Any Verdict Yet?" *Econometrica,* Vol. XXVIII, October, 1960.

17. ——. *Econometric Models and Methods.* (New York: John Wiley and Sons, 1966).

18. Cicchetti, C.J., Seneca, J., and Davidson, P. *The Demand and Supply of Outdoor Recreation.* (New Brunswick, N.J.: Bureau of Economic Research, Rutgers University, 1969).

19. Cochrane, D. and Orcutt, G.H. "Applications of Least Squares to Relationships Containing Autocorrelated Errorterms." *Journal of the American Statistical Association,* Vol. XLIV, March, 1949.

20. Conover, W.J. *Practical Non-Parametric Statistics.* (New York: John Wiley and Sons, 1971).

21. Copas, J.B. "Monte Carlo Results for Estimation in a Stable Markov Time Series." *Journal of the Royal Statistical Society,* A, Vol. CXXIX, 1966.

22. Cox, D.R. *Analysis of Binary Data.* (London: Methuen and Company, Ltd., 1970).

23. Cragg, J.G. *Small Sample Properties of Various Simultaneous Equation Estimators: The Results of Some Monte Carlo Experiments.* Research Memorandum No. 68, Princeton University, October, 1964.

24. ——. "On the Sensitivity of Simultaneous-Equations Estimators to the Stochastic Assumptions of the Models." *Journal of the American Statistical Association.* Vol. LXI, March, 1966.

25. ——. "On the Relative Small-Sample Properties of Several Structural-Equation Estimators." *Econometrica,* Vol. XXXV, January, 1967.

26. ——. "Small-Sample Performances of Various Simultaneous-Equation Estimators in Estimating the Reduced Form." *Metroeconomica,* Vol. XIX, May–August, 1967.

27. ——. "Some Effects of Incorrect Specification on the Small-Sample Properties of Several Simultaneous-Equation Estimators." *International Economic Review,* Vol. IX, February, 1968.

28. ——. "Some Statistical Models for Limited Dependent Variables With Application to the Demand for Durable Goods." *Econometrica,* Vol. XXXIX, September, 1971.

29. Dhrymes, P.J. "On the Treatment of Certain Recurrent Non-Linearities in Regression Analysis." *Southern Economic Journal,* October, 1966.

30. ——. "Efficient Estimation of Distributed Lags With Autocorrelated Error Terms." *International Economic Review,* Vol. X, February, 1969.

31. ——. *Econometrics.* (New York: Harper and Row Publishers, 1970).

32. ——. "A Simplified Structural Estimator for Large Scale Econometric Models." *The Australian Journal of Statistics,* Nov., 1971.

33. ——. *Distributed Lags: Problems of Estimation and Formulation.* (San Francisco: Holden-Day, Inc., 1971).

34. ——., Klein, L.R., and Steiglitz, K. "Estimation of Distributed Lags." *International Economic Review,* Vol. XI, June, 1970.

35. ——., and Pandit, V. "Asymptotic Properties of an Iterate of the Two-

Stage Least Squares Estimator." *Journal of the American Statistical Association,* Vol. LXVII, June, 1972.

36. Dutta, M. *Introduction to Econometric Methods.* Forthcoming, 1972.

37. ——., and Lyttkens, E. "Iterative Instrumental Variables Method and Estimation of a Large Simultaneous System." Discussion paper, Department of Economics, Rutgers University, January, 1970.

38. ——., Smith, V.K., and Loeb, P. "An Evaluation of Alternative Estimators in the Context of a Simultaneous System With Structural and Predictive Criteria: A Monte Carlo Study." Presented to the European Meetings of the *Econometric Society,* September, 1972.

39. ——., and Su, V. "An Econometric Model of Puerto Rico." *Review of Economic Studies,* Vol. XXXVI, July, 1969.

40. Fair, R.C. "The Estimation of Simultaneous Equation Models With Lagged Endogenous Variables and First Order Serially Correlated Errors." *Econometrica,* Vol. XXXVIII, May, 1970.

41. ——. *A Short-Run Forecasting Model of the United States Economy.* (Lexington, Mass: Heath Lexington Books, 1971).

42. Fama, E.F. "The Behavior of Stock-Market Prices." *Journal of Business,* January, 1965.

43. Farrar, D.E. and Glauber, R.F. "Multicollinearity in Regression Analysis: The Problem Revisited." *Review of Economics and Statistics,* Vol. XXXXIX, February, 1967.

44. Feldstein, M. "A Binary Variable Multiple Regression Model of Analysing Factors Affecting Perinatal Mortality and Other Outcomes of Pregnancy." *Journal of the Royal Statistical Society,* Series A, 1966.

45. Ferguson, C.E. and Moroney, J.R. "Efficient Estimation of Neoclassical Parameters of Subsitution and Biased Technological Progress." *Southern Economic Journal,* Vol. XXXVII, October, 1970.

46. Fisher, F.M. "On the Cost of Approximate Specification in Simultaneous Equation Estimation." *Econometrica,* Vol. XXIX, April, 1961.

47. ——. "The Relative Sensitivity to Specification Error of Different k-Class Estimators." *Journal of the American Statistical Association,* Vol. LXI, June, 1961.

48. ——. "The Choice of Instrumental Variables in the Estimation of Economy Wide Econometric Models." *International Economic Review,* Vol. VI, September, 1965.

49. ——. "Near-Identifiability and the Variances of the Disturbance Terms." *Econometrica,* Vol. XXXIII, April, 1965.

50. ——. *A Priori Information and Time Series Analysis.* (Amsterdam: North Holland Publishing Co., 1966).

51. ——. *The Identification Problem in Econometrics.* (New York: McGraw-Hill Book Company, 1966).

52. ——. "Aggregate Production Functions and the Explanation of Wages: A Simulation Experiment." *Review of Economics and Statistics,* Vol. LIII, November, 1971.

53. Glahe, F.R. and Hunt, J.G. "The Small Sample Properties of Simultaneous Equation Least Absolute Estimators vis a vis Least Squares Estimators." *Econometrica*, Vol. XXXVIII, September, 1970.

54. Goldberger, A.S. *Econometric Theory*. (New York: John Wiley and Sons, Inc., 1964).

55. ———. "An Instrumental Variable Interpretation of k-Class Estimators." *Indian Economic Journal*, Vol. XIII, 1965.

56. ———. *Topics in Regression Analysis*. (New York: MacMillan Company, 1968).

57. Goldfeld, S.M. and Quandt, R.E. *Nonlinear Methods in Econometrics*. (Amsterdam: North Holland, 1972).

58. Griliches, Z. "Distributed Lags: A Survey." *Econometrica*, Vol. XXXV, January, 1967.

59. Haavelmo, T. "Methods of Measuring the Marginal Propensity to Consume." *Studies in Econometric Methods* (Chapter 4), Edited by Hood, W.C. and Koopmans, T.C., Cowles Foundation, (New York, John Wiley and Sons, 1963).

60. Haitovsky, Y. "Multicollinearity in Regression Analysis: A Comment." *Review of Economics and Statistics*, Vol. LI, November, 1969.

61. ———., and Jacobs, S. "Regen-Computer Program to Generate Multivariate Observations for Linear Regression Equations." *Annals of Economic and Social Measurement*, Vol. I, January, 1972.

62. Hammersley, J.M. and Handscomb, D.C. *Monte Carlo Methods*, (New York: John Wiley and Sons, 1964).

63. Handscomb, D.C. "Monte Carlo Techniques: Theoretical". in *The Design of Computer Simulation Experiments*, Edited by Naylor, T.H., (Durham, N.C.: Duke University Press, 1969).

64. Hannan, E.J. "The Estimation of Relationships Involving Distributed Lags". *Econometrica*, Vol. XXVI, October, 1958.

65. Hendry, D.F. and Trivedi, P.K. "Maximum Likelihood Estimation of Difference Equations With Moving Average Errors: A Simulation Study." *Review of Economic Studies*, Vol. XXXVIII, April, 1972.

66. Hoch, I. "Simultaneous Equation Bias in the Context of the Cobb-Douglas Production Function." *Econometrica*, Vol. XXVI, October, 1958.

67. Huang, D.S. *Regression and Econometric Methods*. (New York: John Wiley and Sons, Inc., 1970).

68. Huettner, D.A. and Verma, H.L. "Choice of Structural Parameter Values in Monte Carlo Studies of Competing Parameter Estimators." Paper presented to 1971 Annual Meetings of the *Econometric Society*, New Orleans, Louisiana.

69. Johnston, J. *Econometric Methods*. (New York: McGraw-Hill Book Company, 1963).

70. ———. *Econometric Methods*. Second Edition, (New York: McGraw-Hill Book Company, 1972).

71. Jorgenson, D. "Rational Distributed Lag Functions." *Econometrica*, Vol. XXXIV, January, 1966.

72. ——. Hunter, J. and Nadiri, M.I. "The Predictive Performance of Econometric Models of Quarterly Investment Behavior." *Econometrica*, Vol. XXXVIII, March, 1970.

73. ——. "A Comparison of Alternatife Econometric Models of Quarterly Investment Behavior." *Econometrica*, Vol. XXXVIII, March, 1970

74. Judge, G.G. and Takayama, T. "Inequality Restrictions in Regression Analysis." *Journal of the American Statistical Association*, Vol. LXI, March, 1966.

75. Kabe, D.G. "A Note on the Exact Distribution of the GCL Estimators in Two Leading Over-Identified Cases," *Journal of the American Statistical Association*, Vol. LVIII, June, 1963.

76. ——. "On the Exact Distributons of the GCL Estimators in a Leading Three Equation Case." *Journal of the American Statistical Association*, Vol. LIX, September, 1964.

77. Kadane, J.B. "Comparison of k-Class Estimators When the Disturbances Are Small." *Econometrica*, Vol. XXXIX, September, 1971.

78. Kain, J.F. and Quigley, J.M. "Housing Market Discrimination, Homeownership and Savings Behavior." *American Economic Review*, Vol. LXII, June, 1972.

79. Kakwani, N.C. "The Unbiasedness of Zellner's Seemingly Unrelated Regression Equations Estimators." *Journal of the American Statistical Association*, Vol. LXII, March, 1967.

80. Kelejian, H.H. "Two Stage Least Squares and Econometric Systems Linear in Parameters But Nonlinear in Endogenous Variables." *Journal of the American Statistical Association*, Vol. LXVI, June, 1971.

81. Klein, L.R. *Economic Fluctuations in the United States.* (New York: John Wiley and Sons, Inc., 1950).

82. ——. "The Estimation of Distributed Lags." *Econometrica*, Vol. XXVI, October, 1958.

83. ——. "Single Equation vs. Equation System Methods of Estimation in Econometrics." *Econometrica*, Vol. XXVIII, 1960.

84. ——. "Estimation of Interdependent Systems in Macroeconometrics." *Econometrica*, Vol. XXXVII, April, 1969.

85. ——. *An Essay on the Theory of Economic Prediction.* (Chicago: Markham Publishing Company, 1971).

86. —— and Goldberger, A.S. *An Econometric Model of the United States 1929–1952.* (Amsterdam, North Holland, 1952).

87. —— and Nakamura, M. "Singularity in the Equation Systems of Econometrics: Some Aspects of the Problem of Multicollinearity." *International Economic Review*, Vol. III, Sept. 1962.

88. Kloek, T. and Mennes, L.B.M. "Simultaneous Equation Estimation Based on Principal Components of Predetermined Variables." *Econometrica*, Vol. XXVIII, January, 1960.

89. Kmenta, J. "Some Properties of Alternative Estimates of the Cobb-Douglas Production Function." *Econometrica*, Vol. XXXII, January–April, 1964.

90. Kmenta, J. *Elements of Econometrics.* (New York: The MacMillan Company, 1971).

91. —— and Gilbert, R.F. "Small Sample Properties of Alternative Estimators of Seemingly Unrelated Regressions." *Journal of the American Statistical Association,* Vol. LXIII, December, 1968.

92. Kmenta, J. "Estimation of Seemingly Unrelated Regressions With Auto-regressive Disturbances." *Journal of the American Statistical Association,* Vol. LXV, March, 1970.

93. ——., and Joseph, M.E. "A Monte Carlo Study of Alternative Estimates of the Cobb–Douglas Production Function." *Econometrica,* Vol. XXXI, July, 1963.

94. Ladd, G.W. "Effects of Shocks and Errors in Estimation, An Emprical Comparison." *Journal of Farm Economics,* Vol. XXXVIII, May, 1956.

95. Larson, H.J. *Introduction to Probability Theory and Statistical Inference.* (New York: John Wiley and Sons, Inc., 1969).

96. Lee, T.C., Judge, G.C., and Cain, R.L. "A Sampling Study of the Proper-ties of Estimators of Transition Probabilities." *Management Science,* Vol. XV, March, 1969.

97. ——, and Zellner, A. *Estimating Parameters of the Markov Probability Model from Aggregate Time Series Data.* (Amsterdam: North Holland Publishing Company, 1970).

98. Leviatan, N. "Consistent Estimation of Distributed Lags." *International Economic Review,* Vol. IV, January, 1963.

99. Liu, T.C. "Underidentification, Structural Estimation and Forecasting." *Econometrica,* Vol. XXVIII, October, 1960.

100. Maddala, G.S. "Simultaneous Estimation Methods for Large and Medium-Size Econometric Models." *Review of Economic Studies,* Vol. XXXVIII, October, 1971.

101. Malinvaud, E. "Estimation et Prevision dans les Modeles Economiques Autoregressifs." *Review of the International Statistical Institute,* Vol. XXIX, 1961.

102. ——. *Statistical Methods of Econometrics.* (Chicago: Rand McNally and Company, 1966).

103. Marcis, R.G. and Smith, V.K. "The Demand For Liquid Asset Balances by U.S. Manufacturing Corporations: 1959–1970." *Journal of Financial and Quantitative Analysis,* 1973, forthcoming.

104. Mariano, R.S. and Sawa, T. "Exact Finite-Sample Distribution of Limited-Information Maximum Likelihood Estimator for Two Included Endogenous Variables." *Journal of the American Statistical Association,* Vol. LXVII, March, 1972.

105. McCarthy, M.D. "Some Notes on the Generation of Pseudo Structural Errors for Use in Stochastic Simultation Studies." University of Pennsyl-vania, 1969, (unpublished).

106. ——. "Notes on the Selection of Instruments for Two Stage Least Squares and k-Class Type Estimators for Large Models." *Southern Economic Journal,* January, 1971.

107. McGillivray, R.G. "Estimating the Linear Probability Function."
Econometrica, Vol. XXXVIII, September, 1970.

108. Mitchell, B.M. "Estimation of Large Econometric Models by Principal
Components and Instrumental Variable Methods." *Review of Economics
and Statistics,* Vol. LIII, May, 1971.

109. Mitchell, B.M., and Fisher, F.M. "The Choice of Instrumental Variables in
the Estimation of Economy-Wide Econometric Models: Some Further
Thoughts." *International Economic Review,* Vol. XI, June, 1970.

110. Mood, A.M. and Graybill, F.A. *Introduction to the Theory of Statistics,*
Second Edition, (New York: McGraw-Hill Book Company, 1963).

111. Morrison, D.G. "Upper Bounds for Correlations Between Binary Outcomes
and Probabilistic Functions." *Journal of the American Statistical Association,* Vol. LXVII, March, 1972.

112. Morrison, J.L., Jr. "Small Sample Properties of Selected Distributed Lag
Estimators." *International Economic Review,* Vol. XI. February, 1970.

113. Mosbaek, E.J. and Wold, H.O. *Interdependent Systems: Structure and
Estimation.* (Amsterdam: North Holland Publishing Company, 1970).

114. Moy, W.A. "Monte Carlo Techniques: Practical." in *the Design of Computer Simulation Experiments,* Edited by Naylor, T.H. (Durham, N.C.:
Duke University Press, 1969).

115. Nagar, A.L. "The Bias and Moment Matrix of the General k-Class Estimators of the Parameters of Structural Equations." *Econometrica,* Vol.
XXVIII, October, 1959.

116. ——. "A Monte Carlo Study of Alternative Simultaneous Equation Estimators." *Econometrica,* Vol. XXVIII, July, 1960.

117. ——. "Stochastic Simulation of the Brookings Econometric Model." in
The Brookings Model: Some Further Results, Edited by Duesenberry, J.S.
(et. al). (Chicago: Rand-McNally, 1969).

118. Naylor, T.H. (Editor). *The Design of Computer Simulation Experiments.*
(Durham, N.C.: Duke University Press, 1969).

119. ——. *Computer Simulation Experiments With Models of Economic Systems.* (New York: John Wiley and Sons, Inc., 1971).

120. ——, Balintfy, J.L., Burdick, D.S., and Chu, K. *Computer Simulation
Techniques.* (New York: John Wiley and Sons, Inc., 1966).

121. ——, Wertz, K. and Wonnacott, T.H. "Methods for Analyzing Data from
Computer Simulation Experiments." *Communications of the ACM,* Vol. X,
November, 1967.

122. ——, ——, ——. "Some Methods for Evaluating the Effects of Economic
Policies Using Simulation Experiments." *Review of the International
Statistical Institute,* Vol. XXXVI, 1968.

123. Neiswanger, W.A. and Yancey, T.A. "Parameter Estimates and Autonomous Growth." *Journal of the American Statistical Association,* Vol. LIV,
June, 1959.

124. Nerlove, M. "A Tabular Survey of Macro-Econometric Models." *International Economic Review,* Vol. VII, May, 1966.

125. Neter, J. and Maynes, E.S. "On the Appropriateness of the Correlation Coefficient With a 0, 1 Dependent Variable." *Journal of the American Statistical Association,* Vol. LXV, June, 1970.

126. Orcutt, G.H. and Winokur, H.S., Jr. "First Order Autoregression: Inference, Estimation and Prediction." *Econometrica,* Vol. XXXVII, January, 1969.

127. Parks, R.W. "Efficient Estimation of a System of Regression Equations When Disturbances are Both Serially and Contemporaneously Correlated," *Journal of the American Statistical Association,* Vol. LXII, June. 1967.

128. Parks, R.W. "Systems of Demand Equations: An Empirical Comparison of Alternative Functional Forms." *Econometrica,* Vol. XXXVII, October, 1969.

129. Patton, R.A. "Bowling Green State University's Statistical Package for Teaching." Mimeo, 1971.

130. Powell, A. "Aitken Estimators as a Tool in the Allocation of Predetermined Aggregates." *Journal of the American Statistical Association,* Vol. LXIV, September, 1969.

131. Quandt, R.E. "Some Small Sample Properties of Certain Structural Equation Estimators." Research Memorandum No. 48, Princeton University, December, 1962.

132. ———. "On Certain Small Sample Properties of k-Class Estimators." *International Economic Review,* Vol. VI, January, 1965.

133. Ramsey, J.B. "Tests for Specification Errors in Classical Linear Least Squares Regression Analysis." *Journal of the Royal Statistical Society,* Vol. XXXI, 1969.

134. ———. "Models, Specification Error, and Inference: A Discussion of Some Problems in Econometric Methodology." *Bulletin of the Oxford Institute of Economics and Statistics,* Vol. XXXII, November, 1970.

135. ——— and Gilbert, R. "Some Small Sample Properties of Tests for Specification Error." *Journal of the American Statistical Association,* Vol. LXVII, March, 1972.

136. ——— and Zarembka, P. "Alternative Functional Forms and the Aggregate Production Function." *Journal of the American Statistical Association,* Vol. LXVI, September, 1971.

137. Rao, C.R. *Linear Statistical Inference and Its Applications.* (New York: John Wiley and Sons, Inc., 1965).

138. Rao, P. and Grilliches, Z. "Small Sample Properties of Several Two-Stage Regression Methods in the Context of Auto-Correlated Errors." *Journal of the American Statistical Association,* Vol. LXIV, March, 1969.

139. ——— and Miller, R.L. *Applied Econometrics.* (Belmont, California: Wadsworth Publishing Company, Inc., 1971).

140. Richardson, D.H. "The Exact Distribution of a Structural Coefficient Estimator." *Journal of the American Statistical Association,* Vol. LXIII, December, 1968.

141. ——— and Rohr, R.J. "Distribution of a-Structural t-Statistic for Case of Two Included Endogenous Variables." *Journal of the American Statistical Association,* Vol. LXVI, June, 1971.

142. Roberts, H.V. "Statistical Dogma: One Response to a Challenge." *The American Statistician,* Vol. XX, No. 4, 1966.

143. Ruble, W.L. "Improving the Computation of Simultaneous Stochastic Linear Equation Estimates." *Agricultural Economics Report No. 116,* Dept. of Agricultural Economics, Michigan State University, 1968.

144. Sargan, J.D. and Mikhail, W.M. "A General Approximation to the Distribution of Instrumental Variables Estimates." *Econometrica,* Vol. XXXIX, January, 1971.

145. Sargent, T.J. "Some Evidence on the Small Sample Properties of Distributed Lag Estimators in the Presence of Autocorrelated Disturbances." *Review of Economics and Statistics,* Vol. L, February, 1968.

146. Sasser, W.E. *A Finite-Sample Study of Various Simultaneous Equation Estimators.* (Durham, N.C.: Duke University Press, 1973).

147. Sawa, T. "The Exact Sampling Distribution of Ordinary Least Squares and Two-Stage Least Squares Estimators." *Journal of the American Statistical Association,* Vol. LXIV, September, 1969.

148. Schink, W.A. and Chiu, J.S.Y. "A Simulation Study of Effects of Multicollinearity and Autocorrelation on Estimates of Parameters." *Journal of Financial and Quantitative Analysis,* June, 1966.

149. Schmidt, J.W. and Taylor, R.E. *Simulation and Analysis of Industrial Systems.* (Homewood, Illinois: Richard D. Irwin, Inc., 1970).

150. Schmidt, P. "Estimation of a Distributed Lag Model With Second Order Autoregressive Disturbances: A Monte Carlo Experiment." *International Economic Review,* Vol. XII, October, 1971.

151. Siegel, S. *Nonparametric Statistics for the Behavioral Sciences,* (New York: McGraw-Hill, 1956).

152. Sims, C.A. "Linear Regression With Non-Normal Error Terms: A Comment." *Review of Economics and Statistics,* Vol. LIII, May, 1971.

153. Smith, V.K. *An Economic Evaluation of Several Econometric Estimators for Simultaneous Equation Systems.* Unpublished Ph.D. dissertation, Rutgers University, 1970.

154. ———. "A Monte Carly Experiment With a Large Macro-Econometric Model." *Western Economic Journal,* Vol. VIII, December, 1970.

155. ———. "Economic Anonymity and Monte Carlo Studies," *Applied Economics,* Vol. III, March, 1971.

156. ———. "A Comparative Tabular Survey of Monte Carlo and Exact Sampling Studies." *Australian Economic Papers,* Vol. X, December, 1971.

157. ———. "The Small Sample Properties of Selected Econometric Estimators in the Context of Alternative Macro-Models." *Review of International Statistical Institute,* forthcoming.

158. ———. "A Note on the Coefficient of Determination With Linear Probability Functions." (Mimeo), 1972.

159. ——— and Cicchetti, C.J. "Regression Analysis with Dichotomous Dependent Variables." Paper presented to 1972 Annual Meetings of the *Econometric Society,* Toronto, Canada.

160. ——— and Fibiger, W.W. "An Approach for Efficient Estimation of State

and Local Government Expenditure Determinants." *Applied Economics,* forthcoming, 1972.

161. —— and Hall, T.W. "A Comparison of Maximum Likelihood versus Blue Estimators." *Review of Economics and Statistics,* Vol. LIV, May, 1972.

162. —— and Patton, R.A. "The Operational Significance of Identification With Restrictions on the Variance-Covariance Matrix." *Metroeconomica,* Vol. XXIII, September–December, 1971.

163. Sonquist, J.A. and Morgan, J.N. *The Detection of Interaction Effects.* Monograph No. 35, (Ann Arbor: The University of Michigan, 1964).

164. Steiglitz, I. and McBride, L. "A Technique for the Identification of Linear Systems." *IEEE Transactions on Automatic Control,* Vol. AC-X, 1965.

165. Strotz, R.H. and Wold, H.O.A. "Recursive versus Non-Recursive Systems: An Attempt at Synthesis." *Econometrica,* Vol. XXVIII, April, 1960.

166. Summers, R. "A Capital Intensive Approach to the Small Sample Properties of Various Simultaneous Equation Estimators." *Econometrica,* Vol. XXXIII, January, 1965.

167. Takeuchi, K. "Exact Sampling Moments of Ordinary Least Squares, Instrumental Variable and Two-Stage Least Squares Estimators." *International Economic Review,* Vol. XI, February, 1970.

168. Taylor, L.D. and Wilson, T.A. "Three Pass Least Squares: A Method for Estimating Models With a Lagged Dependent Variable." *Review of Economics and Statistics,* Vol. XLVI, November, 1964.

169. Telser, L.G. "Iterative Estimation of a Set of Linear Regression Equations." *Journal of the American Statistical Association,* Vol. LIX, September, 1964.

170. Theil, H. *Principles of Econometrics.* (New York: John Wiley and Sons, 1971).

171. Thomasian, A.J. *The Structure of Probability Theory With Applications.* (New York: McGraw-Hill Book Company, 1969).

172. Thornber, H. "Finite Sample Monte Carlo Studies: An Autoregressive Illustration." *Journal of the American Statistical Association,* Vol. LXII, September, 1967.

173. Tintner, G. *Methodology of Mathematical Economics and Econometrics.* International Encyclopedia of Unified Science, 1968.

174. Wagner, H. "A Monte Carlo Study of Estimates of Simultaneous Linear Structural Equations." *Econometrica,* Vol. XXVI, January, 1958.

175. Walker, S.H. and Duncan, D.B. "Estimation of the Probability of an Event as a Function of Several Independent Variables." *Biometrika,* Vol. LIV, 1967.

176. Wallis, K.F. "Lagged Dependent Variables and Serially Correlated Errors: A Reappraisal of Three-Pass Least Squares." *Review of Economics and Statistics,* Vol. XLIX, November, 1967.

177. ——. "Some Recent Developments in Applied Econometrics: Dynamic Models and Simultaneous Equation Systems." *Journal of Economic Literature,* Vol. VII, September, 1969.

178. Wold, H.O.A. "A Generalization of Causal Chain Models." *Econometrica,* Vol. XXVIII, April, 1960.

179. Wold, H.O.A. "A Fix-Point Theorem with Econometric Background I - II." *Arkiv for Matematik,* Vol. VI, 1965.
180. Wonnacott, R.J. and Wonnacott, T.H. *Econometrics.* (New York: John Wiley and Sons, Inc., 1970).
181. Yancey, T.A., Bock, M.E. and Judge, G.G. "Finite Sample Results for Thiel's Mixed Regression Estimator." *Journal of the American Statistical Association,* Vol. LXVII, March, 1972.
182. Zeckhauser, R. and Thompson, M. "Linear Regression With Non-Normal Error Terms." *Review of Economics and Statistics,* Vol. LII. August 1970
183. Zehna, P.W. *Probability Distributions and Statistics.* (Boston: Allyn and Bacon, Inc., 1970).
184. Zellner, A. "An Efficient Method of Estimating Seemingly Unrelated Regressions and Tests for Aggregation Bias." *Journal of the American Statistical Association*, Vol. LVII, June, 1962.
185. ———. "Estimation of Seemingly Unrelated Regressions: Some Exact Finite Sample Results." *Journal of the American Statistical Association,* Vol. LVIII, December, 1963.
186. ———. *An Introduction to Bayesian Inference in Econometrics.* (New York: John Wiley and Sons, Inc., 1971).
187 Zellner, A. and Huang, D.S. "Further Properties of Efficient Estimators for Seemingly Unrelated Regression Equations," *International Economic Review,* Vol. III, September, 1962.
188. ——— and Lee, T.H. "Joint Estimation of Relationships Involving Discrete Random Variables." *Econometrica,* Vol. XXXIII, April, 1965.
189. ——— and Thiel, H. "Three Stage Least Squares: Simultaneous Estimation of Simultaneous Equations." *Econometrica,* Vol. XXX, January, 1962.

Index

151

About the Author

V. Kerry Smith received his undergraduate degree from Rutgers University in 1966 and a Ph.D. in economics from the same institution in 1970. Since 1969 he has served as an Assistant and Associate Professor of Statistics in the Department of Quantitative Analysis and Control at Bowling Green State University. In 1971 he took a leave from Bowling Green to join Resources for the Future, Inc. as a Visiting Scholar for two years. At present he is completing a monograph for Resources for the Future on technical change and environmental resources. In September 1973 he will join the Department of Economics at the State University of New York at Binghamton as an Associate Professor. His primary fields of interest are econometrics, microeconomic theory and environmental economics. In addition he is the author of several journal articles.

DATE DUE

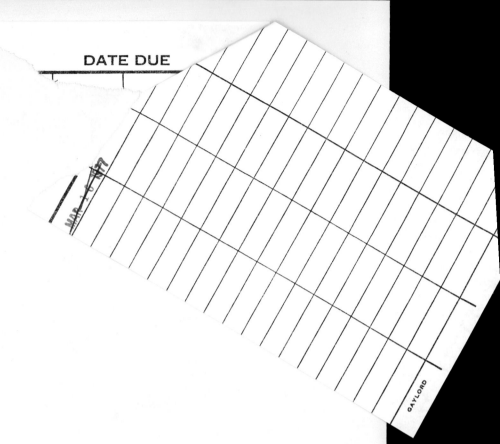

MAR 1 0 1977

GAYLORD

Randall Library – UNCW
HB74.M3 S53   NXWW
Smith / Monte Carlo methods: their role for econom

304900172445$